WHY
ARE YOU
TELLING
ME THIS?

WHY ARE YOU TELLING ME THIS?

A Brief Introduction to Communicating

MARK HICKSON

WHY ARE YOU TELLING ME THIS?
A BRIEF INTRODUCTION TO COMMUNICATING

iUniverse books may be ordered through booksellers or by contacting:

iUniverse
1663 Liberty Drive
Bloomington, IN 47403
www.iuniverse.com
844-349-9409

Because of the dynamic nature of the Internet, any web addresses or links contained in this book may have changed since publication and may no longer be valid. The views expressed in this work are solely those of the author and do not necessarily reflect the views of the publisher, and the publisher hereby disclaims any responsibility for them.

Any people depicted in stock imagery provided by Getty Images are models, and such images are being used for illustrative purposes only.
Certain stock imagery © Getty Images.

ISBN: 978-1-6632-4748-3 (sc)
ISBN: 978-1-6632-4749-0 (e)

Library of Congress Control Number: 2022920414

Print information available on the last page.

iUniverse rev. date: 11/22/2022

CONTENTS

Contents

PROLOGUE

I have taught college courses in communication for more than half a century. When I first started teaching, people asked me what I majored in, and I told them. The usual response was, "I guess I'd better watch what I am saying." I felt that response was somewhat shallow because communication extends much further than correct grammar and pronunciation. I went on to graduate school to major in broadcasting. When people asked me what I was majoring in, I told them—radio and television. The usual response was, "I have a TV at home that doesn't work. Could you fix it?" Once again, I knew nothing about fixing a television; instead, I learned about radio and television programming, economics, and production. I went on to major in interpersonal and organizational communication. It was sort of back to where I had been. It's where I am now minus the organizational part.

I have tried to write a book about my experiences and my knowledge to help people understand one another. It may help you as a speaker or talker, but the primary intent is that it will help you as a listener, a responder, or just as a person.

One of the books I read a long time ago was called *How to Read a Person Like a Book* (Nierenberg and Calero 1971). It was mostly about nonverbal communication or body language, an area of communication that had become popular in the late sixties. The title sounded like something everyone needed to know. I think the authors had a great idea, but we know that we cannot read a person like a book for a variety of reasons. Our insights just are not that good. But we can learn more about them if we take the ego blinders off ourselves and make listening with four senses a higher priority.

To make the point a little bit more, there was a film several years ago called *What Women Want* (2000) with Mel Gibson and Helen Hunt. In the film, Gibson could read women's thoughts but only because he had fallen and hit his head. I suppose the premise is that one of the repercussions of falling is that you may hit your head and gain an insight into the thoughts of the opposite sex. I seriously doubt how realistic that is as well. This book will not teach you to read a person like a book or even how to read a woman's thoughts. It will help with both.

The insights we have into others' intents appears to come in "flashes." I suggest that notion early in this book. Flashes are probably correct more often than not. In this book, we provide some examples that we hope will help the reader increase the percentage of accurate "guesses" about others. Only through learning to use empathy in practice can we become better communicators and communicatees.

Although my wife, Nancy Dorman-Hickson, and longtime colleague, Don Stacks, were instrumental in the writing of this book, I am responsible for the stories and the content, which is the reason it is written in the first person.

I also appreciate the help of Julie Dutton, who proofed the last stages of the book, as well as those at iUniverse who assisted in bringing this book to fruition.

MHIII
Hoover, Alabama

CHAPTER 1

APPROACHING ONE ANOTHER IN REAL LIFE: BEFORE THE FIRST IMPRESSION

Hundreds of self-help books have been on the market for decades. They range from religious authors who write about getting in touch with a higher power as well as health enthusiasts who recommend dieting to improve one's physical attractiveness. One supposedly improves the spiritual well-being, and another improves the physical. There are even books about organizing your closets to enhance your self-concept. Still others teach you to throw some of your possessions away to provide more comfort for your psyche.

This book is an outline of how you can learn to analyze your everyday interactions with other people. It may relieve some stress, but its purpose is to provide analyses to help you spend your time with better results by facing one basic concept. The concept is that self-awareness and the knowledge of reciprocity and synchrony can help you understand what others mean.

You may ask why you need to learn to do this. You are likely to be successful at home and at work if you can. Also, many of our anxieties are precipitated by our bad record of predictions of others' actions. You probably will have less stress simply because you change your expectations of others.

For example, when you ask someone out, you expect (predict) the person will answer in the affirmative. In most cases, if the prediction was for a negative answer, the question would never be asked. When we turn in a report at work, we expect (predict) the boss will be pleased. When the predictions are inaccurate, we fret over how we could have better transmitted the message or written a more substantial report. The fretting is part of the anxiety.

Interestingly, most people believe they are good at communication. Most *believe* that they listen well, although they *know* they don't. This is especially the case when we consider that listening is more than an auditory exercise. It involves looking, thinking, smelling, touching, and even on occasion it involves tasting. In most of these interactions, we begin the process with an initial interaction with a stranger.

In 1972, Leonard and Natalie Zunin wrote a book entitled *Contact*: *The First Four Minutes.* Many of the readers of the book, and there were many, became concerned about the first impressions they made on others and were somewhat alarmed by what they found. That conclusion was based on the notion that it is virtually impossible to see ourselves as others see us.

Although I had just begun studying the body language elements of communication, I felt that analyzing first impressions was something I especially needed to learn. The authors of *Contact* wrote that most first interactions with people lasted four minutes. Within that time frame, others made a set of inferences or assumptions about us. So instead of focusing on the first impression that I make, I started looking at others to see if I could predict which ones could be approached at a party, and which ones seemed to transmit a positive as opposed to negative first impression.

That book reminded me of my first visit to a psychiatrist in Jackson, Mississippi.

It was during the Vietnam conflict. As a potential draftee, I was sent (twice) to take a physical at the military recruitment office in St. Louis. Both times I failed those tests. My failure was of no particular concern because I held a student deferment. My status remained student. I had failed the tests because of high blood pressure. At that time, I had been recently married, moved to another state, lived in a mobile home, feared the military conscription, and I was working on my doctoral dissertation with minimal success. There were good reasons for having high blood pressure. Without completing my dissertation, I moved to Mississippi and took a professorial position.

Six months later I completed my dissertation, and two weeks after that I received a cordial letter from Uncle Sam. I appealed my cordial conscription invitation based on my horrible and extreme high blood pressure (sarcasm intended). The surgeon general allowed the appeal but required me to retake the physical in Jackson, Mississippi. He didn't send me to a cardiologist, though. Instead, he sent me to my first-ever appointment with a psychiatrist. Once the psychiatrist met me, we shook hands. He immediately said, "You bite your fingernails. And your palms are sweaty." He then asked me a series of Freudian questions, implying that I was afraid to go to war. (In Mississippi, that was an unheard-of notion.) A few weeks later, I was in the army, after receiving my lucky selective service lottery number, twenty-one.

It was interesting to me how the psychiatrist, who was obviously paid by the army, made such an evaluation. He never took my blood pressure. But he rated me as military ready. That "interview" took longer than four minutes. However, I am sure that much of his evaluation was based on bitten fingernails and sweaty palms. (There was also, of course, the unforgivable fact that I had never been hunting with my father.)

More recently, Sybil Carrere and John Gottman wrote in 1999 that we make extremely fast evaluations of other people. This is popularly known as "thin slicing." This process takes less than three minutes. Malcolm Gladwell (2005) has suggested that we make such decisions almost intuitively. Or so we think. It may be that our brains are faster than we think. Though this seems like rapid-fire psychology, thin slicing is frequently noted in other fields as well as in popular media.

QUALIFIERS AND DISQUALIFIERS

Sociologist Murray Davis (1973) wrote that we evaluate these first impressions about others based on what he calls qualifiers and disqualifiers. Of course, we all assess others with *different* qualifiers and disqualifiers. In the popular television program, *Seinfeld*, the regular characters created a myriad of disqualifiers. The "low talker" who virtually whispered when talking was necessarily a disqualifier to the regular characters on the television program. There was also the "close talker," who stood too closely when talking. Jerry, the star, was disqualified by one potential suitor based solely her *perception* that Jerry picked his nose once. That one time was enough for Seinfeld to be disqualified, even though he claimed he was not picking his nose. Other factors, such as extreme southern accents, were disqualifiers for the New Yorkers in the television program.

Even as a southerner, as a freshman in college, I found myself infatuated with a very attractive waitress at the Varsity restaurant. One morning at breakfast, the beautiful woman started talking. It was all over. Her southern accent was too strong even for a native Georgian.

Disqualifiers may be more important than qualifiers because with job applications, the potential employer's process is one of elimination. In a sense, we are more concerned about "keeping" one who turns out to be a bad worker than eliminating a good worker using some disqualifier that later may appear to be less negative or irrelevant. I have known of cases where a person was disqualified for a position because he ate a ham and cheese sandwich with no condiments on the bread. Another was almost eliminated because the interviewer didn't like his wife. In a sense we take a "safe" approach that eliminates those with disqualifiers more than we select for qualifiers, especially when the qualifying aspects are similar.

In the beginning, disqualifiers are almost exclusively nonverbal in nature. We may eliminate a person from consideration because she is too tall or too short, too old or too young, too tan or too light, the wrong race, the wrong gender, wearing clothes that do not match our taste, has bad breath or body odor, the wrong color of hair, bad posture, or a loud and obnoxious laugh. Certainly, many of us automatically disqualify one with a disability or stigma. Some of these factors are changeable (hair color, clothing) and others are not (height, weight). Other disqualifiers involve potential interaction, such as between a 6'2" woman and a 5'2" man. Of course, all of this is politically incorrect, but it happens. If the heights are reversed, we apparently consider that less important. A 6'2" man with a 5'2" woman seems to be a less important disqualifier. In the moment we forget that it's unlikely we'll have to listen to the obnoxious laugh often. We may rarely see the candidate's spouse. We may rarely have lunch together again. But that initial interaction with another person is conspicuously salient at the moment, and that moment determines the next step in their career.

In today's electronic world, dating sites include all sorts of "information." Whether the data are true or reality based is a different question. But the dating sites do include pictures. Scammers obviously don't use their own pictures. But sometimes, others use pictures that are ten or fifteen years old. Someone who is adept at creating dating profiles takes the time to provide a picture that makes them appear attractive. One executive of a dating website analyzes this problem differently (Rudder 2014). He writes that if someone sees your picture on a dating site, the adept electronic wizard will look for it in other places such as social media or Google images. Of course, if the two ever meet, they may be surprised. They may not be able to find one another with any more expediency than finding Waldo in the 1990s.

There is a quality called "the handicap principle" in which someone, primarily male, takes on some appearance that is unusual to attract females. The principle exists in other animals also, but in humans a man might have excessive tattoos or piercings. He may wear unusual clothing. The handicap is used to make the male look or appear different. Talking very loudly could be considered a handicap as well.

Back to the assumptions. Most likely we do not consider the context of why a person looks as he does at that moment. For example, I recall a student who came to my 8:00 a.m. class. The other students and I started sniffing around the room because there was an unpleasant smell. Apparently, the student noticed and framed the issue. He apologized but went on to explain that he had to milk the cows right before he came to class. At that agricultural school, the explanation was completely believable. The framing may not have helped his case much, but it did add context. We are all aware of the sniffing that dogs and cats do. We are thankfully less obvious than they are. But if we use the olfactory metaphor as a method of assessing others it applies to us as well. In those first three or four minutes we are sniffing one another to determine whether we ever want to have another conversation with that person.

Commercials on television and the Internet offer us various products to eliminate body odor and bad breath. We have no such product to help us assess these unsanitary factors in others.

SNIFFING

When we meet a stranger, we essentially engage in a sniffing exercise. The bad breath and obvious body odor are literal. In addition, there are metaphorical "sniffs" that we utilize. Ultimately, we want to determine whether we will get along with one another. In life, we go even further. We want to predict whether we can trust the other person. With a potential friend, we want to be able to count on the person. The means by which we do this "sniffing" are verbal and nonverbal.

Alan Garner (1981) has indicated that we can start a conversation with one of three topics: the situation, the other person, or ourselves. Most of us probably use the third option because we know more about ourselves, but the more effective conversation starter might be to ask a question about the other person. I ask my students to complete an index card on the first day of class to gather some basic demographic information. One of the questions that they answer is to indicate their hometown.

I live in a medium-sized city in Alabama. Neither the town nor the university provides a mecca for most travelers from around the world. Thus, when a student answers that she is from Australia or New Zealand, I typically ask her if she is an athlete. This may not sound like a natural progression. But this is my reasoning. I am not aware of any general university recruitment efforts Down Under. Depending on how tall the woman is, I may ask if she is on athletic scholarship. I may guess at which one based on physical factors that apply to different sports. It is also noteworthy that we do not have many foreign students. Those we do have possess particular reasons for choosing our institution. I am often right about their being athletes, and frequently right about the sport.

If I undertook this process in the normal way, I would ask the person where they are from. This is a question that we have asked strangers for a long time. When I was in college at a university in Alabama, the in-state students asked where I was from. I said that I was from Georgia. That answer was typically sufficient for about half of them. But I recall the follow-up from one student. He asked where in Georgia. I answered, "Fort Valley." He then responded, "Hmmm [meaning he had never heard of the place]. What is that near?" I responded, "Macon." Because he apparently had no connection to Macon, he then asked how far my hometown was from Atlanta. I answered that it was about a hundred miles. His next question was really the one that made my day. "I know someone from Atlanta, do you know …?" These initial questions are intended to discover some commonality. He was seeking a way to carry on a conversation. If the question is about an occupation, it may be even more difficult. I was once at a party that was hosted by a professor, and most of the guests were professors. I did run into a man whose wife was a professor. He said he was a wildlife ranger. I knew practically nothing about that. It ended the conversation rather than pushing it forward.

HOMOPHILY

The percentage chance of my knowing someone from Atlanta—one hundred miles away—who lived in a city of more than a million, must have been infinitesimal. But the student asking me the question was not thinking statistically, he was trying to create what researchers call *homophily*. A simplified definition is that homophily is perceived similarity. We seek homophily so that we have something to talk about that we can share. The idea is that opposites do not attract. Similarities more often attract. Most of the research on this topic states that there are at least three types of similarity. They are physical, background, and attitudinal.

As mentioned, we first analyze physical appearance. What we are looking for is someone that we place in the same general category as our own. Height differences and weight differences come into play. There are individual prejudices or preferences for hair color and hair style. Most of the time we first assess whether the other person is male or female. Usually this is a fairly easy first step. However, I have a friend who went to a honky-tonk bar in the 1970s. He had long, blond, flowing hair and wore jeans and a shirt. One of the regular customers came up from behind him and tried to kiss him, thinking that he was a woman. My own story of this first impression was in a restaurant in New Orleans about the same time as my friend was approached. I noticed a woman at the table next to mine who was absolutely beautiful. When she talked, her voice was deeper than mine. I had met my first transgender person in that restaurant.

But that first step of gender evaluation is most often easier than some other factors. The next step is to make some kind of eye contact. Unconsciously, perhaps, we try to determine whether the other person is interested in conversation. We predict that if the other person makes eye contact, we will not be completely rejected. These mutual gazes are essentially sizing up the other person. Reciprocity is the key to making the process work. A gaze becomes a glare or stare when it is not mutual. Nonverbal reciprocity is frequently referred to as synchrony.

These nonverbal efforts require only seconds to perform. In a sense, the eye play is intended to determine whether the other person is interested. Because it is so early, a rejection is not really a rejection.

CONTENT ANALYSIS: MATRIX MATCHING

Once there is some determination of reciprocity, we begin matching one another for homophily. This process typically requires some minimal conversation. A few years ago, I wrote that such an evaluative process is relatively simple (Hickson 2013). The internal messages are: (1) I like that (2) I want that (3) for a certain time frame (4) framed with some intensity. The intensity might be described in terms of "I like her," "I really like her," I REALLY like her."

Homophily itself is the basis of much of this matching. What I have referred to as a matrix goes like this. It may well be that I like the other person's accent. At least it is in the acceptable range of accents for me. But when I measure content, the talk itself may be beyond my range. For example, while it may happen that an engineer and an artist talk with one another, there is significant doubt about whether it will be a long-term relationship. It is at this point in my lectures that students question me for my stereotyping. For me and for this book, we will not think of stereotyping per se as being negative. Stereotyping is simply the early measuring of probabilities. The main reason that I question the engineer-artist relationship is that they typically communicate differently.

When we run into a barrier like this, we begin to measure the qualification against the disqualification. In addition, though, we might try asking questions from a different perspective. We might focus on how each one decided on his or her vocation. In the process, we may find that both were in their high school band. Thus, we may shift our questions from attitudinal homophily to background homophily. They may enjoy the same video games regardless of their vocational interests.

In most studies of homophily, the matrix is a relatively small group of questions and answers. It is like a Rubik's Cube with six sides but only a block or two. If we think of it as a much more complex cube, perhaps with cubes inside of the cubes, we begin the process of seeing other people as much more complex. We move from having a few categories (race, sex, nation of origin, religion) that we may be stereotyping. Individuals are individuals. They are not just part of two or three groups. The matrix is illustrated in Figure 1 (below) in which the upper, right-hand cube can be divided into cubes. The process can even continue into more and more cubes.

Figure 1. Rubik's Cube Inside of a Rubik's Cube

If we think of the high school marching band, the main thing we know is that the other person was not an athlete. This is because one cannot play the trumpet and tackle the running back at the same time. And we know that band members have a certain camaraderie that may not be present on the football team, which may have a different kind of camaraderie. For example, one group is competitive every week, the other usually is not. Neither is a band member a cheerleader. They may lead cheers, but they are not cheerleaders. But like the football team, the band members travel together. They wear uniforms. They must coordinate their work. They are group members.

The background question about whether I was a band member appears to be more precise than where geographically the person is from. As far as geography is concerned, I have lived in the southern United States almost all my life. When I lived in Georgia, people talked about how superior they were to people in Mississippi and Alabama. When I lived in Mississippi, the people there talked about how superior they were to people in Alabama. This goes on and on. Yet in my decades long living in all three of them, I haven't found a dime's worth of difference. Now is someone from Minnesota different from someone who grew up in Georgia? You bet. Because southerners don't have to endure the harsh winters that a Minnesotan might endure. Shoveling snow is part of one's culture in Minnesota. In Georgia, they just let it melt.

But band members from a high school in Minnesota and one from Georgia are probably quite similar. The conversation can continue when specific instruments are discussed. It doesn't even seem to matter that they were in a band decades ago or states away or that they have not picked up that instrument since high school. The culture is still there. The general direction of this approach is an attempt to find greater commonality. It is to move toward communication. Once some homophily is reached, the participants move toward credibility.

CREDIBILITY

Credibility is assessed using at least three, and possibly four factors. One is trustworthiness. In a sense, trustworthiness is about predictability or reliability. Does the other person appear to be consistent in what she says? The second is intelligence. Of course, different people have different requirements. But if we go back to the engineer and the artist, how much does the other person know about his field? (This may be difficult to measure if you are relatively ignorant of the field yourself.) In addition to one's selected vocation, we can look at other types of intelligence. Does the other person have problem-solving skills that help make her relatively independent? Does she have a knowledge of current events? Does he recognize different types of intelligence in others? Does she ask good questions? The third element in credibility is character. Do you think this person is a moral person? How would he decide between two actions? What values does she have?

The fourth possible element in credibility is authenticity. This is sometimes difficult to assess. It usually means that we think the other person is doing and saying what he or she believes to be true. Once we have a basic knowledge of credibility, if it is still positive, we move to interpersonal attraction.

It is at this stage that we attempt to determine "I like that" or "I don't like that." Some of this is based on homophily. For example, a naive person and a cynical person may not match. In any case, authenticity is about whether we think the other person is being "phony." This is perhaps the most intuitive of the four elements. It may or may not show up at all in the first interaction. Because people typically have a first interaction playbook, they may say things to try to "agree" with the other person rather than disagree, and often they fake this agreement. This approach probably works in the beginning, but it is less likely to work for a long-term relationship.

OVERVIEW

You should get from this that this book is not so much about what *you* say or do as it is how you assess others—how well you listen and predict. Most self-help books provide guidance about what you say. Here we are discussing how you analyze others in everyday life. It may be applicable, too, to how we view media people or politicians, but our focus is with everyday life. The first step in learning about this is to look at times and places where you have been "right" about another person and when you have been wrong.

One might ask, why is this important? It is important because relationships are not "me" based. Reciprocity and synchrony are the keys. It is important to know whether there is reciprocity. I asked my students once how many times they would ask someone out, be rejected, and still try again. One of them answered, without hesitation, "Nine." That's plain too many. In this book, we hope to provide guidelines about how to assess reciprocity. In that way, we know whether to continue trying. With such a tool, you should be able to tell if someone likes you and if they will go out with you. When you apply for a job, you should know at the end of an interview question whether you expect to be hired. Obviously, there are other factors in all these things, but this book is to help you raise your batting average. It starts with learning how to listen with all five senses.

CHAPTER 2

THE STORY ABOUT THE GIRL SITTING IN THE BOOTH: THE ART OF "QUICK EMPATHY"

My friends and I were sitting near the bar having after-work drinks in a Mississippi college town's favorite lounge. We were the only customers except for a woman I noticed sitting in a booth seat in the dimly lit bar— more than twenty yards away from where we were. Her age and attire suggested she was a college student. An empty glass was on the table before her, and she was reading something. From its appearance, I knew the item wasn't a book, but could tell little else. I wondered why she was sitting so far from the bar and idly thought perhaps she was waiting for someone. If so, she chose her seat poorly. She would be difficult to spot by anyone entering the dark bar. Additionally, she did not have her sights directed toward the only entrance to the bar.

In short, her waiting behavior seemed to make no sense.

A couple of hours passed. The solitary woman did not order another drink. The barmaid did not approach her. Somewhere during that time, I began to suspect something was wrong. I mentioned my misgivings to my friends. "If you want to talk with her, go ahead," one said, apparently mistakenly translating my concern to that of a desire to flirt with her.

I did nothing. We left. The next day the local newspaper featured a front-page story about the young student. Moments after we left the bar, she shot and killed herself.

I have always had a habit of observing others. I was the kid at the birthday party who quietly assessed the other children's interactions before

I opened my mouth. I'm still that guy. I'm also the fellow who doesn't mind waiting for someone in a mall or waiting for my flight to depart at an airport. I'm content as long as there are people to watch while I wait. When I became a communication teacher, the nature of my "people watching" changed. It intensified, became deeper.

As an academician, I enjoy theory. But for me, discovering the practical application of a communication theory is as exciting, if not more so, than the pursuit of strictly intellectual concepts. In other words, I like to validate an idea in everyday life. I think most people do, in or out of a classroom. Focusing on observations and consequences became a major part of my career as a university professor. I began to study how others in academia reported their own observations or people watching, a term I must admit probably started with zoologist Desmond Morris (1967, 1977).

On his website, Malcolm Gladwell, the author of popular book *Blink*, describes his concept of "rapid cognition" as the "two seconds" that provide the "kind of thinking that happens in the blink of an eye. When we meet someone for the first time, or walk into a house that we are considering buying, or when we read the first few sentences of a book, our mind takes about two seconds to jump to a series of conclusions" (Gladwell 2005).

In this book I present perceptions based on my own personal experience as well as the work of others. I have chosen the word "flashes" to illustrate a point beyond Gladwell's "blink." A flash, as I am using it here, is more involved than a blink. A flash refers to rapidly evaluating alternative or differing explanations of behavior *and* deducing or choosing the most likely conclusion of that behavior. The plural "flashes" indicates more than one in a less-than-organized manner. Think of flashes this way: what we see is not always well organized or structured, but rather more like a pile of photographs in no particular order. Yet, retrospectively, we may integrate these flashes into an organizing album that makes sense of the puzzle.

In the 1960s, I began reading the work of Canadian native Erving Goffman, a sociologist who spent most of his academic life at the University of Pennsylvania. Although he was not the best of writers, Goffman excelled at observing humankind. A colleague of mine who attended social events with Goffman described the sociologist as one who "just sat around and observed." But "just" sitting around and observing is not as easy as it might seem. Sometimes, observation—what might be called the "work of looking"—and not acting properly on what we see or interpret about the situation can have dire consequences as was the case with the woman at the bar (Goffman 2010).

In the case of the woman at the bar, I don't know if my inaction had consequences because I don't know if I could have said or done anything that would have changed her mind about taking her own life. She had been rejected from medical school, according to the newspaper account, citing that fact as her apparent motive. And the item I saw her reading? Her letter of rejection from the medical school.

It is impossible to read people's minds. Nevertheless, we can pinpoint inconsistencies. I knew it was inconsistent for a person to be unsociable while sitting in a place created for sociability. Even when one visits a bar to drown one's sorrows, misery usually loves company. Perhaps that is why bartenders have a reputation for (and are stereotyped as) being good listeners.

The length of time for a flash varies. The entire episode at the bar from start to finish lasted less than three hours. To understand that something is a flash, it's good to develop a keen sense of observation. Learning to be observant and trusting your impressions can help prevent mistakes in communication—or promote communication when there is a lack of it. Observations can help prevent repeating mistakes, as we use our communication skills to connect with each other.

On occasion, we may be able to predict such an occurrence, even though we may be unable to affect it. In a car crash, for instance, we often "know" it is going to happen a second or two before it happens, but by then it is too late.

Could I have done anything about the suicide victim? Perhaps, if I had followed through with my concerns about her. I feel bad about it forty years later, but nothing changed what happened. Like many others, I did not have enough confidence in my reads. She and I were focused on different things, and we had different distractions. We needed to be on the same channel.

In the encounter I mentioned, some of the participants presented images that weren't "authentic." What I mean by that is that the people did not seem genuine, sincere, or unrehearsed. For example, the woman at the bar was not "acting" like a suicide victim, assuming our notion of what that looks like—distraught, hysterical, or noticeably depressed—are accurate.

FAKING IT

As a professor, I've witnessed deception ranging from fraternities sharing old tests to reports illegally obtained online. My wife, a professional writer, has seen writers engaged in plagiarism and others falsifying travel expense reports. Identity theft and the scams perpetuated by professional con artists are examples of illegal deception. In entertainment it can be the dramatic act played by a professional wrestler or the lip synching of a singer. Certainly, actors practice a type of deception. But the kind of deception I am talking about is *everyday deception*—a deception that is neither professional, illegal, and rarely even unethical.

Many of these types of fabrications are benign. They are not intended to harm anyone, even the "victim." Examples of playful deceit (for fun) include the practical joke or a surprise party.

There are also *strategic hoaxes*. I'll give you an example from my own experience. On a night flight from Atlanta to New York, we were in the midst of a thunderstorm that included high, gusting winds. About halfway to our destination, the plane was struck by lightning. All the lights inside and outside of the plane momentarily flashed off then immediately came back on. The flight attendants stopped doing their duties, strapped themselves in, and sat completely still while a hush fell throughout the plane. No one, passenger or staff, said a word. After a brief pause, the flight attendants began moving around the cabin again. About thirty minutes later, the pilot announced, "Ladies and gentlemen, a few minutes ago [thirty!] our plane was struck by lightning. This is no problem, however, as our planes are built to withstand these occurrences. Because of the weather, though, we will be arriving late. Currently we are number forty-four in the landing pattern." This last part made me feel no better. If you consider that landings and departures alternate with one another, this meant there were at least eight-eight planes in the vicinity of La Guardia, in addition to those flying to and from other airports in the region. But the verbal message from the pilot and nonverbal behavior of the airline crew was intended to make us feel better. The pilot's assurances were a strategic hoax used to calm the passengers in a critical situation. As we analyze the communication of others, we need to take note of whether others are being authentic or simply playing a role.

OFF (AND ON) THE BEATEN PATH

People often refer to the spiritual choices they make as "paths" they've taken. I'm proposing something more mundane here that is still a large part of our lives.

Perhaps it is a natural tendency for us not to want to feel trapped by others or circumstances. In the grocery store, for example, we hypothesize which line will take the least amount of time. Once in line, we place a plastic bar between our groceries and the items of others to separate ourselves in every way possible. If the line is too long, we may even express almost silent contempt or anger toward the other customers who may be taking "too long." And we may feel the same way about the store management for not opening another line. Similar types of behavior occur in traffic jams (sometimes even going beyond the contemptuous to road rage). However, if one of the store customers or drivers stares at us, we smile or considerably reduce our contemptuous response. Such actions and their reversals, referred to as "saving face," have become part of our repertoire of deception.

What's happened is that we are frustrated and angry that others have intervened in our paths. As we travel around public and private places and spaces, we move ourselves to get where we want to go, obviously, but also to get others out of our way. At a party, for instance, people try to find and maintain their own comfort zones. Some may move around at the party, trying to locate the perfect spot where they feel comfortable. One reason for moving is to create a path that is itself comfortable where they control their encounters and interactions. They seek out some others—those that are popular or already established as friends, for instance—and *avoid* others—people they don't care for or people that they don't know. Still others at this party hang out near the drinks and food. Most likely they realize that being there places them in a power position. Think about it.

17

Virtually every person attending a party eventually visits the refreshment table. By standing near the refreshments, you ensure that others will come to you.

Besides irritation at the delay, one reason many of us become troubled in a traffic jam is that we perceive the other drivers as "taking up *our* space" or in essence "trapping" us. One of my college roommates was so annoyed at being hemmed in by traffic that he devised a deceptive plan to avoid it. Before attempting to exit the parking lot at a crowded football game, he had his girlfriend stand in front of their car and look on the ground as if looking for a contact lens so that the other drivers would stop. Their delay allowed him to pull out of his space and into the lane. He and his girlfriend deceived the other drivers. (No doubt he risked road rage retribution at this trick.)

In an elevator, we know that the limited space we find ourselves in is temporary. Yet, with each added passenger, we feel the need to redivide the space with an imaginary line so that we maintain our fair share. The actual elevator space does not change. But we deceive ourselves into believing that we can continue to maintain a certain amount of space no matter how crowded the elevator becomes.

Goffman wrote about the importance of taking turns. That's a concept that goes along with this notion of keeping our own space intact and keeping our pathways "fair." He said that turn taking "requires not only an ordering rule but a claiming mechanism as well." What does that mean? An example would be the little dance two people do when they meet on a narrow sidewalk. They must decide who goes first. How they decide that nonverbally—direct eye contact, a shrug to indicate "no, you go first," those types of behaviors—is the claiming mechanism.

Acoustic violations have been discussed by Goffman as well. From a baby's crying in a restaurant to someone's choice of music in an open-windowed car, there have always been violations of one's audio space. Because of the use of cell phones, at no time in history, perhaps, has acoustic violation been as prevalent as it is today. Cell phones ring (or whatever the phone's ringtone equivalent is) in restaurants, meetings, hospitals, schools, places of worship, buses, planes, and concerts. Not only do recipients of these calls allow their phones to ring in inappropriate places, but some also answer and continue conversations in these settings.

They disregard previous codes of privacy and public sound expectation. While the viewpoint of a caller may be that they are merely contacting someone from afar, the onlookers or "onlisteners" often view these calls as interfering with their own spatiotemporal areas. Because of other more natural noises present, the recipient often talks loudly. The person nearby can almost always hear at least one side of the conversation, and in many cases, the other side as well. While a natural assumption may be that it is only the caller's and the recipient's privacy being sacrificed, the reality is inappropriate cell phone usage affects the privacy of others nearby as well. It is almost as if the recipient of the call feels more present with his phone partner than with those in the actual physical environment.

THE WAITING GAME AND BEING BORED

For whatever reason, much of our society has determined that appearing to be bored and waiting are two behaviors that a "normal" person never wants to convey. "Normal" is characterized as that which is acceptable and appropriate. Waiting in a physician's office can be frustrating. Yet most patients attempt to portray the idea and image that they are not waiting, or, if so, that waiting does not bother them as much as it does others. They "cover up" the behavior of waiting by reading or pretending to read magazines that are months out of date. Others look at their cell phones. Poorer actors constantly look at their watches. Often people scan the room to determine who is waiting in the least appropriate fashion.

In a plane that is waiting for the last passengers to board, those already seated skim the plane's safety rules although they have seen or read these pamphlets dozens of times. That's because reading in public is acceptable. Waiting is not. Being bored is not. There are also those in the plane vigorously using their computers or making cell phone calls before the flight attendant tells them to shut down all electronic devices. These travelers have important last-minute work to do before the plane departs—or they want others to think they do. Others place their luggage in bins above the seats. They sit down for a few minutes, get back up, take something out of their bag and place it back in the bin.

Why? Because no one wants to be bored or appear to be bored. We don't want to wait, and we don't want to appear to wait. Doing so makes us seem as if we're not as important as others—or not smart enough to have avoided waiting.

Traffic jams cause us to have to wait. Depending on how long a jam lasts, some drivers drive on the side of the road to "get ahead" of others. Some blow their horns. Some get out of their cars and look ahead as if they knew what caused the jam, they could fix it. I have even seen several drivers adjacent to one another get out of their cars and carry on a conversation.

Society has also determined that people in public should never appear to be alone. Many of us take something to read when we eat alone; others watch television if it's available, regardless of what's being televised. What we are doing is attempting to carry on "normal" appearances.

EVERYDAY COSTUMES

Normality is portrayed through one's dress and appearance including cosmetics, eyeglasses, and physical stigmas such as limps or birthmarks. Such normal appearances are related to one's situation and its context. For example, a male speaker presenting at a convention might wear a suit and a tie, carry a briefcase, etc. The same professor would not appear "normal" if he were to attend his children's soccer match or go to the beach in the same clothes he wore at the convention.

Years ago, I watched a television program called *Identity* hosted by Penn of the magic duo Penn and Teller. The contestant tried to sort out the identities of twelve preselected people. Two things soon became blatantly obvious. First, it was clear the game creators had tried to make the game easy for the contestants. Second, it was certain the contestants were stereotyping. For example, in one program, there were two muscular African American male participants who were to be identified. There was also a short white man who appeared to be non-American by stereotypical standards, such as the hue of his skin, hair, and eyes. One of the professions to be linked with a person was that of a professional football player. The contestant narrowed that possible identity to the two large black men.

Now let's suppose the creators of the program wanted to make the contest difficult. If they had, the professional football player could have been the 5'6" Bosnian, about thirty years old, weighing about 160 pounds—the kicker. Who would ever have thought of the kicker?

Typically, it seems, most people go straight to the stereotype. Stereotyping makes life easier. Perhaps if the TV program proved anything, it showed that the worse the contestants did in their selections, the less prejudices they held. But it seems the producers were trying to deceive the audience into believing that stereotypes are always accurate. Correct answers rewarded that belief.

We look for deceit among others. For example, when waiting in line at the ten-items-or-less counter at the grocery store, we may count the number of items in the cart ahead of us to see if that person is violating the rule. We suspect deception in others. We watch closely as we remove our shoes in line at an airport. We know that airport security is there to uncover potential terrorists. Like the security people, we watch for someone who might be from the Middle East carrying a hidden bomb. We delude ourselves into thinking that we can spot something out of the ordinary, signs that announce, "I'm a terrorist!" But does any of this make sense? Wouldn't a terrorist work at fitting in and avoid the very stereotype that he or she knows exist in those who would thwart his or her efforts?

It is not that we say and do "normal" things but rather that we try to appear normal. So, what about that little old lady with the Southern accent? Could she be a terrorist? What about the seven-year-old with the stuffed bear? Recently, the Transportation Security Administration (TSA) personnel have been chastised for giving the same attention to passengers who don't have stereotypical characteristics in large measure to avoid the charge of racial profiling. One reason for this chastisement is that the public at large *wants* a stereotype. An interesting note is that profiling would probably be acceptable in many people's minds if it were based on behavior and not physical appearance. Pulling your hair out? Singing, screaming, or otherwise making a spectacle of yourself? Thanks for making it obvious. You're loony and clearly need to be searched and detained.

Recently the TSA began a program at Logan Airport in Boston that adds to the security clearance process by questioning passengers. In addition to body X-rays and the removal of shoes, now passengers must answer such inquiries as "Where are you traveling?" and "What's the purpose of your trip?" The agents are not looking for flubbed answers. They seek involuntary physiological "tells," such as perspiring in a cool room, signs that might indicate nervousness or hidden secrets. If the agents suspect deception, they detain the passenger for further inquiry. The record of these detentions in finding terrorists is not good.

Even those of us who aren't trying to blow up a plane tend to disguise who we are. For most of us, this means transforming ourselves to appear more attractive, younger, or sexier.

Many of us seek to weigh less or at least to appear to weigh less. "Sucking-in" products such as Spanx, like what used to be called a girdle, are readily available. These cosmetic devices fit the idea of deception as opposed to the more difficult weight-loss solution of exercise. But regimens, equipment, and other facets of the megabucks industry that fall under the category of "exercise" often fall under the auspices of deception as well. "You too can have this perfect 'ten' body by spending only ten minutes a day using our product!" hawks the TV commercial. In addition, we now have curling irons to make hair curlier and straightening irons to make hair straighter. How can we forget the hair growing concoction as seen on TV a few years ago? The actual results resembled black paint sprayed directly on a balding (and deluded) head. We also have "genuine" (faux) diamond jewelry.

But it's not just diet pills, girdles, hair paint, or fake rings. There is also surgery to enhance the breast, the face, the lips, and so on. We have hair coloring products and contact lenses that change the color of the iris. Add bikini waxes, facelifts, hair rollers, makeup, nail polish, piercings, tattoos, haircuts and hairpieces, padded bras, tanning beds and lotions, and elevator shoes to the long list of deceptive products of which we avail ourselves.

SPIES AMONG US

Most of us, to some extent or another, practice deception. In some ways, the "normal" person's dip into deception has made the task of actual espionage more difficult! The epitome of a spy stereotype was generated in the 1960s. He was, of course, "Bond, James Bond," the 007 agent with a license to kill—not to mention being suave and debonair at all times. Bond then (and now) was an impossibly cool guy in a cool car wearing a tuxedo while climbing a mountain to rescue the vamping victim from the jaws of the communist dragon (or some other evildoer). The media had a field day when they discovered real-life spy Valerie Plame. She fit the female equivalent of a fantasy stereotype. The blond with the long glossy hair and designer suits testified before Congress about her being "outed" as a spy. Her drop-dead looks made her seem more vamp than a CIA agent. At one point, I served in the army's military intelligence. Therefore, I can say with some certainty that most agents more closely resemble Donald Rumsfeld than Valerie Plame ... or James Bond.

Nevertheless, researchers like Goffman provide us with a complete set of descriptions of how we try to fool ourselves and other people. We want to believe that we are indeed the always-in-control movie star rather than the stuttering geek with adhesive tape on his Buddy Holly-like, black-rimmed glasses. We want to be Bond, James Bond, not Herman, Pee-wee Herman.

We adapt our physical appearance for several reasons. First, we may change our appearance to create attractiveness. Second, we may modify our appearance to increase power. Third, we may transform our appearance to create avoidance.

As a freshman in college, I remember trying to add a course on registration day. The lines were quite long. But I noticed that there were some male students dressed in coats and ties who walked to the front of the line, presumably because they were working in some official capacity at the event. The departmental representatives immediately gave them whatever they asked for. "How unfair!" I thought at first. Soon, however, I decided to take advantage of the situation. I walked across the street to my apartment and changed from my casual summer clothes to an appropriate white shirt, tie, and navy blue jacket. I walked back to the front of the registration line and asked for the card I needed. I received it with no questions asked.

CREATING A PHYSICAL APPEARANCE

Like a good con artist, we analyze our audiences to seek a means of functioning that appears to be acceptable. In a sense, we are all actors operating in brief movies, television shows, and commercials. We even perform in short plays, many of them rituals such as greetings, farewells, "making up," "holding grudges," "starting something," and the more formal ones such as births, graduations, weddings, and funerals. We most often serve as our own playwrights and some of us are even the producers, creating the overall "tone" of the drama, including what Goffman called its "key." The trick is to know whether we are in a combat movie, a romantic comedy, or an epic with a moral!

As teenagers, girls may modify their appearances to look older and more attractive by increasing their breast size—not through surgery but with a padded bra. To appear older, boys sometimes add artifacts such as smoking cigarettes. They may also try to increase their height by putting lifts in their shoes or wearing cowboy boots with heels.

Plotlines for many a program or book portray people with glasses as nerdy and asexual. But some people may intentionally select eyeglasses instead of contact lens to create an appearance of being a serious intellectual. Some people purposefully wear clothing that hides their natural body shape, making their physique appear as a blob whether or not it really is. Such dress often serves as a protective maneuver to thwart unwanted attention or attraction from others.

Perhaps the ultimate in deceptive communication occurs on the internet. We can now offer a completely different face as well as a different personality and claim either as our own to web viewers—perhaps the one we want or the one we think others want us to have. So is the teenager who creates a Facebook page with a false name, picture, and bio.

OBSERVING FLASHES

A first thought about observing flashes might indicate that we are waiting for breasts or sexual parts to be unveiled. That is not the case here. This book is about human behavior and communication, not psychology. What messages do others send us? Do they intend to send that message? How can learning to observe people's communicative behavior help us with our own?

Finally, the philosophical question: how real are we? Hopefully, we can become better at making that determination through looking at flashes.

OVERVIEW

Many of the decisions we make every day are subconscious choices. But we want to be in control, so we create a path for ourselves that makes sense to us. Someone else may block the paths we choose. We use costumes, cosmetics, and even posture to deceive others into thinking that we are smarter than we really are, dumber than we really are, taller than we really are, shorter than we really are, more fit than we really are, more friendly than we really are, etc.

We perform these acts and make such choices because that's what society has told us is "normal."

CHAPTER 3

THE STORY ABOUT THE GUY AT THE SPEECH: WHY SOME PEOPLE TALK TOO MUCH

My wife and I attended a dinner presentation at a hotel in Birmingham, Alabama, where Shelby Foote, the noted Civil War historian, was the speaker. We stood in line near the banquet room, waiting for a table to be assigned to us. There were about a hundred people in the line, and most were carrying on relatively quiet conversations, introducing themselves to those in front of and behind them. We noticed one large man in his late thirties. He was dressed in coat and tie, like almost all the men there. However, something simply did not fit. He was walking around, shaking hands, and speaking loudly as he introduced himself and greeted people in the line. His relatively loud, vocal tone and his gestures were more like a blue-collar worker, but he was dressed in white-collar attire. To an outside observer, the man appeared to be a television stereotype of a southern sheriff. It was almost as if he felt uncomfortable wearing the suit. It was obvious to all who saw him that he was a talker.

Each of us can become a talker from time to time, but we know that the serious talker is almost *always* talking. What do they talk about? Most frequently they talk about themselves, but there are variations on the theme. They are unavoidable. It is as if they *must* talk to breathe. For some, talking is merely a means of gaining attention as an outcome. Our friends and colleagues, Jim McCroskey and Virginia Richmond (1993) coined a term for them—"talkaholics." They are labeled talkaholics because their behavior is analogous to "alcoholics" or "workaholics." These people engage in obsessive, compulsive behaviors. Just as a workaholic may stay at her office fifteen hours a day, and an alcoholic keeps a pint readily available, talkaholics either talk or ready themselves for talk constantly.

Georgetown University linguist Deborah Tannen (1990) provided considerable research on the topic. In her book, *You Just Don't Understand*, Tannen explained in detail some differences in male and female communication. One of the first issues she discussed was who talked more, men or women. If you ask that question of a group of a hundred people, the response is about fifty-fifty. Generally, men think women talk more, and women think men do. But there are exceptions on both sides. According to Tannen, there is a reason for the discrepancies. She writes that one talks more depending on the situation. Women talk more in private, and men talk more in public.

When we encounter someone like the man at the Foote presentation, we tend to hypothesize about them. The man at the hotel could have been a politician or a salesman. To this day, I do not know his name or his profession. But I do know that he enjoyed talking. Before we sat at our table before the speech, I predicted to my wife that this very man would ask a question following the speech if allowed to do so. We sat at our table and lost track of the target man. Mr. Foote concluded his speech and asked if there were any questions.

In this situation, most audience members are reluctant to ask a question, but not the bombastic talker. The man I had noticed was the *first* to ask a question. The preface to his question took several minutes, and then he asked his one-sentence question. He stood up, said his name. He was sitting in the center, the table directly in front of Foote. His question, of course, had already been answered in the speech. But Mr. Foote was kind in not pointing out that fact. Perhaps it was Foote's experience in making such presentations that he knew such questions were probable.

At the conclusion of Mr. Foote's answer, the man in the audience had completed his mission. He was assured that everyone there knew that he had been there, and he could go home and sleep well. The question is what was his mission? His mission was to gain attention. He did not have a good question and probably had not listened that well to the speech because his entire focus since leaving his home had been to gain attention at the presentation. Could the other people standing in line have predicted his asking a question? I am certain that many of them could have. Foote could have and probably did.

But the inquiring man at the dinner is not unusual. We see these talkers when we watch congressional hearings in Washington. When asking a witness a question, a congressperson prefaces the question with about 80 percent of his or her allotted time, sometimes not allowing time enough for the question to be answered. But the congressperson probably does not care about the witness's answer. Sometimes there is no question at all. At some point, there will be a printed record of the hearings, and everyone who reads the record (as well as those who watched on television) will know that Congressperson X was there, and he or she asked a question.

The preface part is significant in these talks. The preface is to create an impression that the talker knows something or is taking a side. They are part of impression management. The people in Georgia want to know that their representative is strong on the military, and those from Alaska want to know their congressperson favors protecting wildlife and the Second Amendment to the Constitution. In addition, of course, a lengthy preface provides more time for talk. This is known as *holding the floor*.

HOLDING THE FLOOR

Gaining attention is a major part of the process of persuasion. The general principle is that if one can hold the floor, the one holding it is in charge at least during that time. Holding the floor has several purposes. First, it allows the talker to say whatever he or she wants to say. Second, it prevents others from saying what they want to say. Third, it gives the impression that the talker knows what she is talking about.

These are also the reasons that most deliberative bodies have rules about holding the floor. *Robert's Rules of Order* and other parliamentary procedures are used to allow different sides of an issue to have equal or almost equal time in presenting their case. The U. S. Senate has a rule that one person may speak as long as he or she wishes unless overruled by a super majority (three-fifths) of the votes. South Carolina Senator Strom Thurmond holds the record for the longest speech (filibuster) at more than twenty-four consecutive hours. He was arguing against a civil rights bill. So how can one hold the floor in other contexts?

One way is to talk loudly and allow no interruptions. In this approach, it is certainly better to stand because one can be louder when standing. There are probably even respiratory reasons for this. Thus, if the person is larger and taller, he has a better chance of holding the floor. But a person can also gain attention and hold the floor through appearing unusual. We all know what it is like when a stunning model appears in the room. Upon entering the room, a model has the floor in most instances. A sense of awe appears on the faces of others in the room. Most know this. She is likely to arrive late so that people notice her early in the meeting.

At times, one must interrupt others to grab the needed attention. In class, many raise their hands. Others wait for a pause. The interruptions themselves, Tannen writes, fall into three categories. A *negative* interruption is an attempt to argue with the previous speaker. A *positive* interruption is an agreement—a yeah, yeah, that's right! A *neutral* interruption is about another topic, like "pass the peas, please." Another form, not mentioned by Tannen, is a *topic-changing* interruption. Here the talker interrupts perhaps because he knows little about the topic being discussed. Thus, he attempts to change the topic to his own specialization. This way he is allowed to talk more.

In each of these cases, whether a speech or a congressional inquiry, the response of the other person is virtually irrelevant. In fact, there may not even be a need for a response or an audience. This type of talk is cathartic; it makes the speaker feel better.

CATHARSIS

Few academics discuss catharsis as a purpose of human interaction. Perhaps this is because there is so little to say about it. Maybe a useful way of thinking of catharsis is to consider it as talking to oneself aloud. This is not to say that others are not around; it simply means that the others are irrelevant. As was the case of the man at the Foote speech, others' listening to him was relatively unimportant. Catharsis, then, is somewhat of an emotional release.

Take a woman at a grocery store. She's in a hurry. In many cases, she is probably in a hurry because she is always in a hurry. She is often in a hurry because she plans poorly. However, none of those factors appear to influence how she talks. She looks at the lines in the grocery store, trying to decide which line might be fastest. People have blocked her self-declared path. Even in the "ten or less" lane there are eight people in line. She first loudly whispers to herself about where did these people come from or why is this store *always* inefficient? After all, there are lanes that are not open.

But whispering to herself is ineffective. Additionally, she wants others to know that she is irritated. She speaks the comments a little louder. Then she asks those in line, "Don't you think they should open another lane?" Yet no one answers. She is not speaking to any of them individually. She is speaking to them in general. Three days later she engages in the same behavior. So why doesn't she ask the management to open another lane? She may, but she probably doesn't. If she did, and they opened another lane, she wouldn't have anything to complain about. It's the process that's important, not the outcome.

Are others irritated? Maybe. Probably. For them, though, this is not a cathartic event. She may be saying what they are thinking, but somehow the others have been socialized not to say everything they think. They may feel she is only making the situation worse. Some places, like government offices, appear to be acceptable places for people to complain. In governmental offices, others may join in the catharsis because after all, *they pay* these people. The employees remember that they are also taxpayers.

I have previously suggested that interaction is like playing tennis, or ping pong, or badminton, or volleyball. Interactions are essentially volleys. Anyone who plays those games knows that there are different kinds of volleys and different reasons for volleying. To interact, to carry on conversation, is more like practice volleying. One is not playing "hard." The important goal is to keep the ball or birdie from going out of bounds. After all, that slows down the conversation and makes further talk awkward.

In a "real" tennis game, the purpose is to win. It is competitive. Thus, a player may hit the ball hard. The player may hit the ball in the far backcourt and on the subsequent shot, barely "drop" the ball over the net, perhaps with reverse spin on it. In this way, the opponent must run hard and still is unlikely to get there. The real, competitive game is like persuasion.

But catharsis is more like practicing by oneself. A player may hit the tennis ball up against a wall. I have seen children numerous times throw a ball at the front steps of their homes and catch their own pitches. The sole player always wins these contests because *there is only one player*.

Catharsis also occurs in the home. A most obvious example is when a couple returns from work. The wife may start complaining about situations at work. "The boss is cruel. There is too much work." Others have been laid off, and the wife has to do two people's jobs. The husband will likely try to find solutions. He wants her to stay in the job, but he wants her to have options. "Could you transfer to another department?" But she doesn't want to hear that. She is not searching for a solution. The husband is assuming she wants to win. She just wants to hit the ball against the wall. The husband, in fact, is the wall. All he must do is to respond in such a way that she can catch her own pitch.

The other option for the husband is to engage in his own catharsis. "The traffic was terrible on 65." And he goes on and on. She complains about work, and he complains about traffic. Never the twain shall meet because they are not trying to communicate with one another. Each one is implementing catharsis. If they had two dogs, each one could talk to one of the dogs. The two soliloquies are separate and distinct.

Catharsis occurs at work but usually not in the workplace. Rather two workers get together for lunch, and the primary topic of conversation is frequently something negative about the coworkers or the boss, neither of whom is there. One might say, "She gives me work at the last minute and expects me to stay late." The other says, "My boss is rarely there. When I have a question, I have to text his cell phone, and he seems irritated." Neither of the workers is searching for a solution. This kind of behavior is likely to reoccur for months, even years. The coworker obviously cannot or will not say anything to the boss. The complaining worker has chosen the wrong target for a solution but the right one for catharsis. Thus, there is a game of two players, each hitting the ball against the wall.

Good counselors are excellent at playing the role of the husband or the coworker in this case. They know that much of what clients (or patients) are saying is cathartic. That's one of the reasons why psychologist Carl Rogers

(1951), among others, advocated a reflective approach to counseling. He suggested that many clients not only know what their problems are, but that they also know the solutions. They simply need a nonjudgmental wall. The counselor paraphrases and reflects to the client what the client said. Other psychologists have even suggested that a good friend makes a pretty good and inexpensive counselor.

Catharsis takes many forms. At one restaurant, I noticed that virtually all the servers used a particular approach when delivering the food to their customers. The server said, "Here is your corn, and peas, and ham, and biscuits." Then the server moved to the other customer and said, "Pork chop, potatoes, peas, and rolls. Is there anything else?" The server takes each piece of food in its container, one at a time. All the time, the server is hoping for no feedback. Feedback, in this case, would mean that there was an error. This talk is essentially self-reflective.

The server is talking to himself. In communication terms, though, it is a way to ensure that the order is correct. The same tactic may be used at a drive-through. Interestingly, some drive-through restaurants have begun writing the order on a small billboard so that the customer can see it as well as hear it repeated.

THE ELEMENTARY SCHOOL TEACHER

I do not intend to demean elementary school teachers here. To me they should be among the most highly respected people in society. However, there is a tendency for them to talk in a certain way. The reason this happens is that elementary school teachers are more like nurturers. These teachers are responsible, in large measure, for society's *socialization*. "Don't hit." "Keep your hands to yourself." "Wash your hands." "Stay in line." "Be quiet." In addition to the basic rules of socialization as content, the method is repetition. Naturally, there is good reason for the repetition. Young children simply do not listen and immediately obey.

Many of these children have heard these rules before from their parents. At home, they probably paid less attention. After all, the home is where one is allowed to break the rules of socialization. "Don't eat with your hands." "Pick up your toys." Frequently, too frequently, the penalty for violating these rules is merely more repetition. "How many times have I told you to tie your shoes?" "How many times?" As parents we cannot to keep count. Parents devise all sorts of penalty and reward measures to work this out. Parents know that their children are not really afraid of them, nor do they want them to be. So, there are star charts on the refrigerator. Rules are posted on the door of the child's room. It is almost like parents are thinking if a military approach doesn't work, perhaps a bureaucratic approach will. If the child cares nothing about the stars, or the parent forgets to add a star, the system is doomed to failure. Thank goodness for the parent, the day finally arises when the child goes to preschool for at least a few hours a day. School gives parents another enforcer and nurturer.

I recall the first day of preschool for our twins, who are now almost thirty years old. I was pleased that they would have something new to do and new friends to meet. Perhaps, too, their teachers would "straighten them out" at least a little. After a few weeks, I arrived at the school to pick the children up after they had completed their half day of "mother's day out." I observed these two- and three-year-olds walking in line down a hallway, not saying a word. I was truly amazed. Perhaps it wasn't so different from the military after all.

Basic military training involves equality. No matter what social class a private is from, he or she is treated the same as the other privates. Penalties are frequently given in mass. That is, if one private gets out of line, the entire unit is punished for it. "All right, everyone give me fifty push-ups!" That order is not delivered in a nurturing way. Hopefully the soldiers and the children also learn that if they do not follow the rules, the other soldiers or children will not like them. Thus, most of them do as they are told most of the time.

At home the parents are unlikely to ask for fifty push-ups. Neither is the preschool teacher going to order them to exercise in that manner. But peer pressure is present in the school, and it is not present at home. The assumption underlying the military approach is that peer pressure is a more effective motivator than repeated orders from an authority, teacher, or parent.

The elementary school teacher encourages students while teaching the power of socialization. It is after all, the education system that teaches socialization as much as parents in the home. The combination of peer pressure and teacher pressure frequently works.

If there is a problem with the nurturing elementary school teacher approach it is that it sometimes cannot be turned off. The teacher is seen frequently "talking down" to the spouse or others in public. "Do you really think you should *eat* that ice cream?" The obvious answer may be no, but adults are frequently irritated by someone's telling them what to do or what to eat. For this reason, we sometimes find ourselves getting irritated at another person because we feel that they are "ordering us around" while the teacher surrogate is merely trying to be nurturing and helpful. The elementary school teacher, then, talks a lot.

THE LONELY ONE

In our society, many of us have jobs that require our being around others seven or eight or more hours a day. In most of these situations, the amount of talk is spread fairly evenly among those who are involved. Others have jobs where they spend most of their time alone, cooped up. When we take these two groups together, one has a need to talk when the job is over, and one does not.

This notion is probably how door-to-door salesmen frequently made their sales in the day when one person in the family stayed home almost all day. The salesmen had a particular method in what we may have thought was their madness. They employed a lengthy spiel about the vacuum cleaner or car they were selling. It was necessary to have a lengthy one because eventually the customer would buy something to get the salesman out of the home. We might refer to this notion as *the inability to say goodbye*.

Like the directors of many motion pictures, it seems that many of us cannot discover a way or means of ending a conversation. A common way twenty years ago was to use the phrase, "I'm going to let you go now." We may have the same kind of problem. At times, neither party wants to take the responsibility for ending the conversation.

THE PARENTHETICAL TALKER AND MAKING SURE TO GET IT RIGHT

There are individuals who are obsessively concerned about the *precision* of their talk. I am unaware whether these personalities are obsessive about anything else. I do know that in their desire to be precise, they become verbose. An example might be: "I was driving to Walgreen's Drug Store ... well, I had intended to go to CVS, but since I also needed to go to the post office, I went to Walgreen's instead, and there I met a former high school classmate ... from Pinson High School, we graduated in 1980, in June ..." In a sense, the talk is not verbose in the traditional sense of simply too many words. Instead, it is *overly content specific.* It sounds like Ernest Hemingway as edited by James Joyce.

As a listener, I must learn to filter most of the parenthetical expressions because they are irrelevant to me even though they are important for the sender's obsessions. It appears that the basic problem is that the talker begins vocalizing before being prepared to do so.

My son returned from elementary school one day. He indicated that he had said something "wrong" to a classmate. I told him he needed to think about what he was going to say before he said it. The next day he talked to me about his experiences in school on that day. He said, "Dad, 'member you said I need to think about what I am going to say before I say it?" I answered in the affirmative. He replied, "Well, that's hard!" For most of us it is difficult. These obsessives with their parenthetical expressions may be the epitome of people with the problem. It also appears that people with this problem have a genetic difficulty. That is, other members of their family tend to do the same thing. At best they are horrible storytellers.

ORAL VERSUS WRITTEN COMMUNICATION

In high school, I was a pretty good writing student. College English, though, squelched my ambition for some time. It was not until thirteen years later that I had my first book published. I do recall several things that writing teachers told us in both high school and college. One of them was to avoid redundancy. Repeating the same ideas over and over bores a reader. I even learned in the Presbyterian Church why our congregations ended the Lord's Prayer with "Forever, Amen." Other Protestant churches said, "Forever and ever. Amen." In the Presbyterian Church, we apparently had more grammarians who thought "forever and ever" was redundant.

"Forever" does sound like a pretty long time. When I decided to major on the "speech" side of English, I discovered that such an observation about redundancy generally does not apply.

When our twins went off to college, I do not know that we repeated that many different messages to them. However, I am certain we have said, "Clean up your room," a few hundred times. I realize that some talkers are excessive about redundancy, but a little redundancy might be a good thing when talking. There are a couple of reasons for this. First, we cannot play back our talk unless there is a video camera around somewhere. Second, listening has become a lost art.

Not only are there listening problems, but also hearing problems in the twenty-first century. I would guess that about half the students in one of my classes wear some kind of earphone to listen to something else as class begins. Most remove them when class starts. Frequently, I can hear the music playing through iPods or iPhones. So hearing is becoming a difficulty for teenagers and twenty-somethings. Those who may be a bit older have the problems too, because they have attended rock concerts or played CDs loud for years. To some extent, I have to lecture to twenty-year-olds as if they were seventy-year-olds.

POWER PLAYS

In my lifetime, I have been to hundreds of meetings. In some cases, the participants were fairly equal in status, and in others there were substantial power and status differences. Many people in these situations try to create power plays by talking when they do not need to do so or shouldn't.

DISTRACTED TALKER

This person is mostly a bad listener, but bad listening may be caused by distractions both within the environment and within one's mind. An excellent example is when people attend conferences, conventions, and mass meetings. In the hallways, people are moving from room to room, usually with about fifteen or twenty minutes of break time to allow for the moves. In many instances, participants will see someone they know in the hallways. They strike up a conversation, but it should be noted that these are not real conversations. Most are looking around to see if there is "someone better" to talk with.

OVERVIEW

Talkers talk for several reasons. First, they cannot help it. Second, they may want to gain attention. Third, they may engage in catharsis. Mostly, though, they do not feel the need to be equal in time when it comes to holding the floor. Their listeners rarely stop them. These are the people we just put up with because they have other positive qualities that outweigh their talkativeness.

CHAPTER 4

LONG AND WINDING ROADS: ANOMALIES OF SPACE

As we begin this journey of insight, we discuss the routes that we take in everyday life. For some reason, at least in American society, we generate plans for the day. The composition of these plans includes how we move from place to place. Efficiency is a mainstay of our culture. It sometimes appears that engaging in our tasks quickly is more important than doing them right. We begin our journey with how London taught its taxi drivers about pathways.

One of the most precise jobs in the world has been the occupation of London cab driver. It's not so much a dirty job, nor is it theoretical physics. But it is difficult. Not only must drivers be safe, but they also must memorize the map of London. It is not one of the easiest cities to learn. It takes most driving students at least two years to pass the examination for certification. Certainly, in today's world with global positioning systems (GPS) for traveling, one would hardly consider knowing directions to be a talent. Apparently, Londoners do. Eleanor Maguire and Katherine Wollett and their colleagues (2000), researchers at University College London, found that the hippocampus in the brain is larger in successful cab drivers than among those drivers who failed the test. In addition, the more experienced cab drivers had larger hippocampi than those with less experience. Their conclusion was that by studying the map in such detail, they increased the size of part of the brain.

Most of us think that there is such a thing as a "sense of direction." For the most part, we feel that we are either born with it or born without it. Maguire and Wollett's work suggests that "path knowledge" can be improved if one works at it. As Gladwell (2000) has directed us, it probably takes at least ten thousand hours of practice.

Paths are important to us. Each day, many of us leave our homes for work. In all probability, we take the same path every day, even if there are others available. In a way, a sense of path is closely connected to one's sense of territory. When driving from home to work, we transport ourselves from one home territory to another. A path, then, is a settled or projected set of directions that one uses to go from one territory to another. A path has at least two purposes. First, it is the most direct way to get somewhere. Second, it avoids barriers (roadwork, traffic, dangerous areas). In fact, many of us listen to the radio or a traffic app on the way to work so that we can hear about where the traffic jams are located and thereby choose an auxiliary path.

When we look for a new restaurant, the complexity of finding it increases without an electronic helpmate. Some search the internet for directions. Usually, the GPS system is helpful. Sometimes, though, we wonder how the GPS people ever decided to go that way.

I remember that a friend of mine lived about fifteen miles away. He frequently invited me to his home. Every time I left to visit, I felt like I was having a new adventure. One might think that I have a horrible sense of direction. In fact, I don't. But I can tell you now, if I were offered $1,000 to drive to his home, I doubt I could find it. Some places are simply harder to find than are others. And, by the way, GPS didn't help.

There are two sets of directions that we use when there is no electronic help. One of the ways is quite like what one might find on Google Maps, though. That is, "Turn left on Highway 31, go a mile and a half, and take a left on 119. At the third traffic light, take a left. Go four-tenths of a mile to Henry Street. Your destination is the fourth house on the right." In some senses, the Google method is the more scientific method.

I refer to the second method as the old country model. "Go to the second red light and take a left. Drive until you get to the Shell station on the right. Take a left. Drive until you get to a big sign that reads, 'Country Manor,' and take a left. You'll see a sign for Henry Street. Your destination is the first yellow house on the right." At times, human direction givers even use history. "Go down the highway, take a left at the fork, pass the Old Gibbons Place, and you know you have gone too far when you reach the former Shell station." The latter works only if you have lived in the county for a decade.

It may be that paths and territory are more than paths and territory. Territory is an important phenomenon in that it has ownership. We think that we own not just a place but also the things that are in it. The "home place" is our "castle." We insure our homes from fire and theft as well as floods. We also insure the contents in the house. Appliances and furniture are included as possessions there. We insure some valuables like jewelry so that when we take them with us, they remain secure.

Frequently, we take our things with us. We put them in the car that we also insure. The inside of the car is our territory, a mobile territory, like our jewelry. Both are valuable and mobile. In fact, we consider our automobiles not only secure but also private. We talk to ourselves—sometimes pretending to be talking to the drivers in front of us. We eat in the car. We drink in the car. We phone in the car. We read in the car. We use the car as a mobile filing cabinet, despite the fact that it may not be very well organized. And, of course, some of us even text in the car.

We place claim on all these possessions. In some cases, we have legal paperwork to prove that the territory belongs to us. While these things are now viewed as status symbols, the original purpose of the home territory was to protect us from other animals and other human beings. Perhaps cavemen kept their clubs close to the entrance of the cave, just as some contemporary natives keep a baseball bat. The caveman likely took much of his meat back to the cave to share and to protect from outsiders as well as sniffing bears. Now we have refrigerators and cupboards in our homes. Instead of the club, we have the home security system and the neighborhood watch—and maybe a bat.

As long ago as the nineteenth century, William James said that part of our very being is the material self. My dad recognized this when I said something was "mine." His response was, "Does it have your name on it?" Usually it didn't, but I wrote my name on as many possessions as I could. Possessions are important to us for a number of reasons, but certainly we feel that they are close to us. As a child, I took my Christmas toys to bed with me. I wanted them close, even during the night when I was asleep.

Many people keep antiques because they are "part of the family." They are handed down for generations. Family silverware is infrequently used, but at Thanksgiving, we remember that the forks and spoons belonged to mother and grandmother and great-grandmother. We have to keep them "close" to the family.

When we think of the government's information, much of it is classified to keep it close. We possess secrets and keep them close. When one discloses secrets, we feel violated. In the case of government documents, it is against the law to disclose much of this information. We have homes, and homes may be more than just a building where we live. Our automobiles are also homes even though we use them to move around. Homes carry territory with them. The territory may be the lot where the house is built or the trunk space in the car. For those of us who still leave the house to work, our space or office at work is also a home territory.

TYPES OF TERRITORY

The first type of territory *is static possessions.* When we first think of territory, we usually start with real property, land. We protect property with fences and hedges, with locked gates, vicious animals, electrical alarms, radios, or televisions that remain on when we are not present, and even fake animals that produce a barking sound. The message we send is, "This is my area within this fence." You are to stay out unless I invite you. We sometimes have our name on the mailbox or on the home. This practice tells both the postal employees and the public at large that this is where my mail goes, and my house is nearby.

The home is important for certain practical events such as eating and sleeping. It is also where we assume significant privacy. We need privacy to protect us from others when we are asleep or otherwise preoccupied with personal issues. The home is the most obvious place for most of our possessions. While the most valuable possessions may be kept in a bank or similar institution, the home frequently is where we keep jewelry, electronic devices, and clothing. Many who do not own a home have renter's insurance for their possessions. Possessions in the home typically remain in relatively the same place for lengthy periods of time.

Second, we have *portable possessions.* We carry these items with us. They may be in a purse, a wallet, a car, or our pockets. Sometimes we take them in briefcases or luggage. These are usually smaller items that we may need to use in variety of contexts. Some officials may have combination locks on their briefcases, and in certain instances they may even handcuff the briefcase to themselves. The most critical portable possessions are keys, wallet, and cell phone.

The third type of territory is *information*. Having one's computer stolen is not as important for the computer itself as it is for the information stored in it. In the old days, people kept their love letters stored away in a box. The reason was not so much that the letters had a dollar value but that the letters were private. Today we have LifeLock, a company that claims to secure personal information, such as social security numbers, passwords, bank account numbers, and credit card numbers so that you can avoid identity theft. While LifeLock does not claim to secure your love letters, they do secure one's financial identity.

The extent to which information is private or secret varies considerably. The personal information described above is considered private by almost everyone. Legally, medical information is considered private, but certainly there are individuals who tell you anything you want to know about their recent surgeries. Because cameras appear to be everywhere from the neighborhood convenience store to high in the sky, we know that we are being watched. But such governmental and corporate vigilance may have been overtaken by cell phones. Virtually everything about us is in the cloud. Even if you are in an intimate situation in a private place, your picture may be taken and posted online without your consent. Frequently, we can be virtually followed as we move from place to place.

Interestingly, banks have tested several different means for customers to access accounts without typing in a number at an automatic teller machine. One possibility is the use of a fingerprint. Another is to use our pupils to identify ourselves. Still another is a voiceprint. None of those methods is in extensive use yet, but the likelihood of some new security in the future is high. Many cell phones now use a thumbprint for access. A new method, being tested in Europe, is using one's perspiration, which researchers claim is as much of a personal identifier as a fingerprint.

Of course, the only place that you can secure your most private information is in your brain. The only way to compromise this privacy is if you provide it yourself. Another person may ask, "What are you thinking?"

In so doing, they may be asking the most personal question of all. Yet we try to ascertain what others are thinking much of the time. In some cases, when they do not tell us, we create thoughts for them. Eventually the banks may just have the customer "think" his or her passcode to enter the ATM.

The next territory is the space directly in front of the ATM that may be called a *niche*. A niche might include a telephone booth, where normal expectations are that only one person will occupy it at a time. In a larger context, but with the same principle, we have a parking space. Parking spaces are reserved for only one vehicle at a time. If two drivers arrive at a space at about the same time, they reasonably expect that they will try to determine who was first and queue in order. The queuing order is important at four-way traffic stops and in some other contexts.

The stalls in bathrooms, and urinals, are also niches. One person is typically allowed at a time. An architect friend of ours determined that queuing in bathrooms is a much longer process for women than for men. Therefore, she plans for two women's restrooms to every one male restroom in sports stadiums.

Much is made of niches at governmental offices, the most common of which is the post office. Interestingly, a line may be just as long at a supermarket, but in governmental buildings we find a plethora of signs— sometimes printed and sometimes handmade. The most common one is, "Stand behind the yellow line until you are called to a window." In so doing, the government employees verbally direct citizens to follow rules that should be a nonverbal custom.

Functional territory is an area that one needs to perform a certain task. Tennis players know that they need more room for their game than simply what is between the lines. They must run around the lines and behind the lines. When a bystander walks or runs behind them, they frequently become irritated. The same is true for golf. No one should get so close that the club could strike him.

We have already mentioned queuing in the context of the niche. This term is quite common in the United Kingdom with roundabouts used in traffic. In the United States, queuing is usually referred to as taking turns. In preschool, taking turns and standing in line are two of the most basic territorial concepts. Teenagers formerly used the concept to stand in line and wait (sometimes for days) to purchase concert tickets. And although we may buy tickets now through a computer or a cell phone app, we still must queue up.

Anytime we phone a company, a doctor's office, or a governmental institution, we are in a *queue*. A typical automated response to a phone call is, "We appreciate your business. We have many callers today. The time expected to answer your call is fifteen minutes. Please hold the line and wait for our representative." This is followed by the playing of some music and advertisements for you to buy more products from the company you are calling to complain about their service.

Like several aspects of space, time is frequently intertwined with the space. A queue, for example, is on a time-space continuum. As we tend to stress because someone may unknowingly be in our path, we must also deal with the formalities of invited guests. There are some guests who are always the first to show up. They are usually the loneliest of your guests. They arrive early to the house and are too anxious to drive around so as not to be the first to show up. For many of these early arrivals, this habit occurs in all their dealings, business or social. On the opposite end of the time continuum, some people are just always late. I have met a number of them. I have not determined why they are always late, but they are. Many are nice people who would never consider themselves rude. But having several people waiting for you, when everyone else is there, is rude.

Table 3.1

Types of Territory

Type of Territory	Examples	Protection	Static or Portable
Static territory	Home	Locks, Fences	Static
Portable territory	Purse, Wallet	On person	Portable
Information territory	Password	Privacy	Portable
Functional territory	Tennis court	Norm	Static
Queuing	Standing in line	Norm/Numbers	Portable
Personal space	Body bubble	Norm	Portable

We must take turns at the checkout counters at various stores. What we know is that the distance we maintain from one another increases from the time we are in elementary school until we attend college. In addition, adult customers are more likely to allow younger children to break in line. Most of us would allow a three-year-old to break in line, but not a twelve-year-old.

One of the interesting aspects of deciding about space is that it appears to be related to the physical attractiveness of the other person. When we consider the other person attractive, we are more likely to allow that person to get closer to us. On the other hand, even when the audience should be aware that only strangers are waiting, we do not want others to think that we are with certain people. Generally, we try to keep a little distance from a friend or relative who embarrasses us. They may not notice.

Personal space or body space is an imaginary territory the surrounds us. When another violates this territory, it may be a serious issue. The amount of space in this imaginary bubble varies. In large measure, the variation is a cultural phenomenon. Americans tend to use more body space than do people from South America and almost everywhere else except Great Britain. In addition, males tend to need more personal space than females do.

We note our need for space when we enter a waiting room in a physician's office. In a pediatrician's office, there are typically two sections of the waiting room—for the sick and the well. Of course, there is good reason to maintain space because there are sick people there. We must avoid germs. And of course, we also may want to avoid people with whom we do not wish to converse.

The physician's office leads us to the most personal of violative space—touching someone's else's body. In the doctor's office, we must remember that this is a physician. She may remain a human being for conversation when the patient is clothed and there is no touching. But when an examination begins, we do not want that person to be a person. We are doctor and patient.

Such professional touching also takes place with those who care for our hair. We would hardly allow others to touch us in the head and neck area normally, as we consider these intimate areas of touch, not much different from the crotch or breast areas.

In the United States, a massage is generally a private matter. However, when I was in Thailand, I found that there were many massage parlors. The parlors are of two types—what we consider here to be of the legal variety and the illegal variety, although both are legal in Bangkok. In the nonsexual massage parlors, there are ten or so tables in an open room, so that ten people may be getting a massage at the same time. Here we do have some chairs in airports and shopping malls where the shoulders are massaged, but we expect privacy for a full massage.

MARKING TERRITORY

Most animals mark their territory. Dogs urinate around their territory to notify other dogs that the space belongs to a certain dog. Most humans have invented more sophisticated systems for marking their territory. We post "no trespassing" signs, we construct fences, we lock our doors, we place name plates on our doors and desks. Types of markers are noted in Table 3.2 (below).

Table 3.2.
Types of Markers.

Type of Marker	Most Common Place	Method
Boundary marker	Athletic courts and fields	Painted or chalk line
	Real property	Fences, hedges, tree lines
	Parking spaces	Painted lines
	Grocery store checkouts	Metal or plastic bars, baskets
	Highways	Center line
Central marker	Bars and lounges	Drink on bar in front of seat
	Restaurants	Backpack in center in front of seat, books
	Entertainment	Program in seat (when no reserved seats)
Personal marker	Office or desk	Nameplate

A real or imaginary line drawn around our territory is a boundary. When we purchase real estate, we hire a surveyor to create or recreate the boundary lines. We pay taxes on the real estate within those boundaries. Fences are frequently built around at least some of those boundaries.

In certain parts of the world, including Brazil and Thailand, bricked or concrete fences have broken glass atop the fence to keep predators out. In the United States, using electricity or barbed wire serves a similar purpose. In all these cases, the owner is telling outsiders that breaking into the property creates dire circumstances for violators.

We even mark temporary territory. We leave a program on the seat to "reserve" it during intermission. We may leave our drink at the bar intending to hold that space when we return. However, we would not leave the drink unless we had someone keeping an eye on the drink for us.

In our offices at work, we have nameplates on doors that indicate that this is somebody's personal space. While not specific to one person, the sign "Employees Only" gives notice that only certain people are to enter. Some people also place their names on cars, drums, and other items.

VIOLATING TERRITORY

Static possessions, like homes and automobiles, must be protected even when the owner is absent. Obvious violations of the home are break-ins and robberies. Lesser violations of the home occur as well. Most of us assume that guests will not be violators, but they certainly can be. Laws about these violations appeared after the norms for privacy and security had already been established.

There are norms for guests in one's home. Most guests ask the owner of the home for permission to use a refrigerator or the bathroom. These areas are considered private. A person would also ask permission to smoke, although in today's world, this would be a rare occurrence. No one would expect a guest to open the doors of closets or to rummage through dresser drawers. However, it is not unusual for guests to go into the kitchen for another beer during a Super Bowl party

Some people violate portable possessions by touching them—such stroking as a fur coat. Still others may violate possessions by holding on to them too long. There are still individuals who feel comfortable touching the stomach of a pregnant woman who would never touch her stomach were she not pregnant. Those with proper etiquette would never do so. After all, what if she isn't pregnant?

On another occasion, I experienced a flash of a different sort with less severe repercussions. A friend and I were in Rio de Janeiro, walking in the neighborhood of Ipanema. Numerous sidewalk merchants solicited customers by yelling at passersby about sales and bargains, not unlike a barker at a carnival. They gestured for us to come close. In the midst of this chaos, two young boys silently began following us. I noticed them when they pointed to our feet. After about twenty yards, one of them quickly ran by and slid his hand in my right front pants pocket and stole the money I had placed there. Then the thieves darted away, down the crowded sidewalk, gone in a flash.

In retrospect, I knew two things. First, I deduced the boys pegged us as tourists by our choice of footwear. Our shoes (not to mention that we were not speaking Portuguese) were not typical of the area. Second, in hindsight, I realized I had a habit of constantly placing my hand in my pocket, checking on my money—and effectively telegraphing exactly where the thief needed to target his efforts. My friend and I nonverbally told the pickpockets exactly what they needed to know: we fit their general target audience (tourists); and I showed them the bullseye (my right front pocket). At least I had the foresight to carry little money since I knew the area had a reputation for pickpockets. The thieves' analysis took only a few minutes.

Could I have done anything to prevent the robbery? I could have worn shoes that blended in. I could have broken my habit of touching to check my money (although these youth unfortunately were most likely professionals in training and knew what they were about). The young thieves were not "acting" like thieves. They didn't have darting eyes and weren't whispering and skulking in a dark alley. Perhaps being in a strange land complicates our searching for flashes.

The latitude that we provide a guest at home depends on the nature of the relationship between the owner and the guest. In our minds, we distinguish among stranger-guests, acquaintance-guests, friend-guests, and family-guests. As we move from one to another, we increase the amount of flexibility of access. A stranger-guest is typically allowed to come to the door, perhaps inside the door slightly. Those doing business may be allowed in the "front room." Fifty years ago, these outsiders may have had access to the kitchen as well. But as door-to-door salespeople have decreased in number, the access has dwindled. The salesman's mantra, "a foot in the door," was really to gain a foot in the kitchen, where they thought sales were more easily negotiated. Acquaintance-guests are allowed in the front room and perhaps in the kitchen or den but not in the bedrooms or even the bathrooms without permission. Friend-guests enter the front room, the den, the kitchen, and may even use the bathroom with just a nod. Guests who are relatives have almost full access to the house depending on how closely related they are to the owner.

In-laws-to-be sometimes go overboard. They may check the bedroom or closets for evidence of the fact that their daughter is living with the potential fiancé. This was a common practice of my father-in-law.

Although more common in automobiles, an auditory violation can occur in the home. A guest might change the music or turn up the volume. Even talking too loudly might be a violation if there are infants in the home or if someone is asleep. Olfactory violations may occur if a guest assumes that he can smoke in someone else's home.

One violates a niche when looking over at another man at a urinal. Certainly, there have been violations by politicians in a stall. In these cases, although the space is public, some expectation of privacy is still the rule.

Functional space can be violated at an ATM. We all have a certain amount of space that we feel we deserve when standing in front of the machine, punching in numbers. At bookstores, some people stand in front of books or magazines for "too long," leaving others to wait. This is also common at a grocery store, particularly at the meat section. Some customers will pick up every steak, looking at it as if there is something substantially different other than the weight and the price. The niche is violated in parking spaces when offenders park "over the line" or "crooked." The elevator is another common spot for violating the niche.

The most common violation of queuing is breaking in line. Although this is a norm, it is often treated as if it were law.

ACOUSTIC VIOLATIONS

We live in a world of sounds and noise. While many of us have difficulty hearing, especially as we get older, some of us have a severe sensitivity to sound (noise). In my office building, the elevator's taped "narrator" tells everyone what floor we are about to arrive at. Cell phones make numerous noises, play various songs, and are personalized with ringtones that are simply obnoxious. Computers make noises from the original "You've got mail" to beeps and even movies playing on them. Vehicles make noises, including the beeping that large vehicles make when backing up. Refrigerators beep to let us know the door has been open too long. Microwaves tell us the food is ready with a beep, and sometimes numerous beeps. Washers, dryers, ovens all have some noise to help us. Most of these are electronic noises. We also have mechanical noises and natural noises such as birds chirping and dogs barking.

Inside the car, there's a beep when the seatbelt is not connected. There is a beep when the emergency brake is on. Sometimes there is a beep when there is not enough or too much air in one of the tires. The acoustic distractions that we live with in today's world are pervasive.

We also frequently hear the music being played in someone else's car that is near us. I am not certain why some people think that everyone wants to hear their music, but they do. Inside the car, a passenger may change the volume of the radio or even change the station. And interestingly, we may turn down the volume ourselves when we are looking for something. This particular action is indicative of the idea that maybe we don't have as much confidence in our multitasking as we think.

Measure that against what I used to hear on the farm. Dogs, cats, chickens, and birds. Most of the sounds were natural sounds.

In a restaurant, there is music, typically loud music. In restaurants, there can be a certain musical identity consistent with the restaurant itself. The Mexican restaurant plays Mexican music, the Italian restaurant has Italian music, the sixties hamburger joint has oldies but goodies, and the Texas steak house has country and western music.

In most restaurants, the music is so loud that most people cannot hear another carry on a conversation. We feel that we must have background music in real life just like we do in the movies. Perhaps the loudest audio violations are at sporting events and concerts. For concerts, these sounds are the entertainment. At sporting events, most of the noises come from electronic scoreboards, not from the fans or the bands.

If we think of sound having a path, it is especially difficult to circumnavigate what I need to hear to get to the destination.

VISUAL VIOLATIONS

Restaurants, too, provide visual violations. In many restaurants today, there are televisions. Most of the televisions carry sports, and some are even called sports bars. These are violations only to the extent that one considers a restaurant a place to eat and carry on conversations. There are particularly distractions for couples in that one of the partners is there to eat and watch the game, while the other is there to eat and carry on a conversation. A real distraction might occur when the partner wishing to watch the game is in a seat where he or she cannot see the television.

If this is supposed to be a "romantic dinner," the sports fanatic might even play along with the seating arrangement. However, this sports person is likely to frequent the restroom with a brief "rest" on the way and on the way back to "check the score." Such restaurants may be responsible for killing the romance at the romantic dinner. The fan may take the cell phone to the restroom to get the score.

For some reason, in recent years, there are visual violations caused by a variety of menus placed on the tables. There is the regular menu which is handed to the customer by the server, but there are also dessert and drink menus that take such space on the table. Add to that a specials menu, which, by the way, does not mean a cheaper menu.

Billboards can be visual distractions in another sense. As if there were not enough distractions, a large billboard can draw our attention away from the task at hand. Puzzling billboards, sexy billboards, and odd billboards tend to do that. They serve their own purpose in drawing attention, but they could be a safety hazard.

51

We are most often distracted by what's new and what's unusual. A motorcyclist without tattoos might be distracting. A bride who doesn't wear a white bridal gown might be as distracting as having the bridesmaids wear white. People with unusual facial hair or who wear unusual clothing (or no clothing) can be a distraction. We may be distracted by extremely attractive or extremely unattractive people walking on the sidewalk.

TOUCH VIOLATIONS

We should remember that America is one of the most touch-free societies in the world. The only common types of touch are handshakes and hugs. Even those have their time and place. Since COVID-19 started in our country in early 2020, space and tactile violations have been made more explicit. The medical experts suggested that we not shake hands, hug, or kiss. Thus, what used to be normal became a violation. Of course, we also have rules and laws about touching other people.

OLFACTORY VIOLATIONS

Any three-year-old can tell you about personal flatulence as an olfactory violation. For three-year-olds, the violation can be of the solid nature as well as gaseous. Some less dramatic violations include a visit to grandma's house. There is a certain odor that smells like grandma's home. Owners of restaurants are cognizant of any olfactory violation that is inappropriate for the situation. Remember, though, there are positive smells as well. We use fragrances to improve the odors in rooms and buildings. And most of us attempt to ensure that we smell good, and we buy toothpaste, mouthwash, aftershave, deodorant, perfume, and body lotion to succeed.

OVERVIEW

It seems that we naturally have a concept of a path to take when we are going somewhere. It is more likely that a path is created by a habit. Once we have established a path for ourselves, we attempt to avoid any barriers to our arriving at the destination. In addition to the path, we have territory that we "own," legally or otherwise. We create markers to let others know how much space belongs to each of us. We need to be aware of potential violators and violations to ensure that our territory is secure.

CHAPTER 5

THE GREENROOM: GETTING OURSELVES "READY"

When it comes to interpersonal relationships, visual observation is important. We look at people to determine who they are. At times when can recognize a friend from tens of yards away. In the criminal realm, some of us are asked to identify a person whom we may have "met" only once. We also desire to know how the other person feels at a particular time. If a friend doesn't speak, we ask ourselves why that happened. We are more aware of this in critical times as when a friend has broken up with his spouse or when a family member passed away. In our careers we spend time practicing for a job interview in the hope that we will give the best impression.

Goffman (2010) developed a schema for analyzing human communication. His approach is called dramaturgical. He indicated that we are frequently (if not always) playing a part in the play of life. In that context we play different roles in different plays. Here we observe how people prepare for these roles. These visual components help us assess a situation. In the field of communication, they include factors that we call facial recognition, facial expression, and physical appearance.

FACIAL RECOGNITION

Most of us take facial recognition as a given. We see other people, and right away, we know whether we know them, or we don't. Only a few times in our lives do we mistake the wrong person for a friend. Oliver

Sachs, a physician, told an incredible story of a man who could recognize his own face in the mirror only because he was the only person in front of the mirror.

Sachs (2010) himself had the disease called face blindness, or prosopagnosia. "People with very severe prosopagnosia may be unable to recognize their spouse or to pick out their own child in a group of others" (p. 87). Sachs asked his colleagues at work to do things like wear the same color tie to work each day so that he knew who it was. He was able to "see" certain things such as a really tall person or a really short person, but he claimed that "average" people were his biggest problem. Heather Sellers, another patient with the same problem, has written that she ran up to her husband, "threw my arms around him and stretched up to kiss him: he drew back pressing me away. It wasn't Dave. I had the wrong guy" (Sellers 2010, 4). Being face blind is like being colorblind.

Obviously, face blindness is a rare disease. However, many of us run into the same problems as Sellers did, just not with a spouse. We have in our minds the faces of hundreds or thousands of people we have met. The task of remembering them all is a difficult one. When we try to recall the name that goes with the face, the task becomes even more monumental. Perhaps we should think of face recognition as being on a scale. On the one end is face blindness, and on the other are those people who never seem to forget a face or the name that goes with it.

A few years ago, I went out to eat with my twin son and daughter. After the server came to our table, my son said, "Wasn't that Savannah?" The server had been one of my students. I had spoken to her but had not stated her name. I told them that it was. I asked my children, who were about seventeen at the time, how they knew her. They said that they had all gone to elementary school together nine years earlier. At my age, I cannot recognize fellow high school students. In addition, I have taught college for half a century, so when a former student asks, "Do you remember me?" most often I admit that I do not. There are simply too many faces and names in my facial encyclopedia.

When we also consider how many faces we have seen in movies and on television, the numbers become quite excessive. When someone speaks to us, we begin looking through our "card catalog" of faces, usually trying to attach some situational context to the face. When we meet one of these people, we should ask for some context so that we are both more comfortable. Once we know who we are talking with, we can begin analyzing other factors such as physical appearance.

PHYSICAL APPEARANCE

Something within us makes us believe that physical appearance is not so important. Perhaps our hearts say so. But our minds know better. Among other things, physical appearance is the number one factor in selecting a first date. And a second date. By the third date perhaps we become less shallow. We accept a less-than-perfect appearance in the other person and realize that we are not perfect either. Or maybe, maybe, we learn not to judge that one book by its cover. In addition to social relationships, physical attractiveness is virtually a job requirement in many professions, including television anchors of both sexes, most actors, and many jobs that require substantial dealing with other people. Almost all of us are aware that physical appearance is a factor in relationships and in our careers. For that reason, we typically try to "put our best face (and body)" forward when we know that we will be evaluated for anything meaningful.

In a theater there is frequently a room near the stage where actors and others prepare for their performances. Although most of us are not actors (at least professionally), we rarely think about this room, commonly known as the greenroom. This is a room, or at least some space, where actors have their makeup applied, dress in their costumes, and psychologically as well as physically prepare for a performance.

In real life, the greenroom is the bedroom, the bathroom, or the car (unfortunately). While each of these places has a primary purpose other than preparing for the real-life play, they are each used to apply makeup or to adjust clothing. In these everyday performances, we are stars in our own show, at least in our own minds.

In the television show I discussed earlier, where contestants attempted to determine the profession of the actors, I noticed that using stereotypes assisted the contestants. In most cases, the stereotypes are somewhat accurate. Quite frankly, Tiger Woods doesn't look like an NFL lineman. Bill Gates doesn't look like a plumber.

The stereotypes also provide us a beginning point as we prepare for our roles. When I was in graduate school, I was determined to be a professor. In the stereotype I created for myself, I felt I had to drink black coffee, wear a beard, and smoke a pipe. Elbow pads on my suit might add the final touch. Of course, not all professors, not even all male professors, engage in such stereotypical behavior. At various stages of my professional career, I did each of those things, but not necessarily at the same time. As we have mentioned, though, a general stereotype may not be accurate. Sometimes our appearance "naturally" creates a stereotype. A muscular guy may appear to be a blue-collar worker, but he may just be someone who works out. Hypothetically, he could be an accountant. In my case, I was trying to "invent" myself into a stereotype.

Today most professors do not wear suits, and even fewer wear ties when they do wear suits. But those who wear suits usually do not look like lawyers who wear suits. For example, sometimes professors' pants and the coat may not exactly match. I once had a colleague whose clothes rarely matched. He was colorblind so blues and browns were frequently mismatched. If another person did not know he was colorblind, that person may have just thought my friend had bad taste. The concept of fashion is typically alien to the academic world. There are exceptions, but few of them. To some extent, though, there is a uniform for whatever we do. Such uniforms are important for compliance, identification, interpersonal attraction, physical acumen, and comfort.

When theater people try to invent professors for stage or media, they use these stereotypes to dress them. A professor in the 1960s may have a ponytail haircut, wear an unbuttoned vest without a coat and bell bottoms. If the actor is to portray a 1980s professor, he may wear the suit and tie. Another factor that theater people may take into consideration is what academic field the actor is portraying. A business professor might wear the coat and tie, whereas the chemistry professor may wear a lab coat. As we mentioned earlier, such stereotypes are somewhat beginning points for our trying to understand the other person.

PHYSICAL APPEARANCE AND COMPLIANCE

Leonard Bickman (1974) undertook research where he tested some of the "uniforms" that we wear. Bickman considered a uniform to be what we wear on a regular basis, even if it is simply a coat and tie. He found that those who wear suits gain more compliance from others than those who appear to be blue-collar workers. At a subway station in New York, Bickman had confederates (male and female) dress in two different ways to try to get an experimental subject to comply with the request. A dime was intentionally left in the coin return of a phone booth. Once a subject went into the booth, the confederate walked up to the door, knocked, and said something like, "I am sorry, could you check to see whether I left a dime in the coin return?" Half of the time, the confederate was dressed in a suit. The other half of the time the confederate was dressed in blue-collar attire. The results were that the dime was returned twice as often to the suited confederate (77 percent to 38 percent). Given those numbers, it seems obvious that if you want someone to comply you should wear a suit. Another interesting finding is that at least 23 percent of the subjects lied about the dime being in the coin return no matter what. In this particular case, though, it may be that the subjects associated the blue-collar confederate with beggars, since subway stations were places frequented by vagrants when Bickman's study was undertaken.

Perhaps for that reason, Bickman tested his findings in other contexts. This time, though, he tested his research on a city sidewalk. The male confederate was dressed in what the researcher called "uniforms." In one case, he was dressed as a salesman, with slacks and a sports coat. In another, he was dressed in an all-white uniform, such as a milkman might have worn at the time For the third uniform, he was dressed as a security guard but did not wear a badge or carry a gun. Two situations were used. First, the confederate "ordered" a passerby to pick up a wadded piece of paper off the sidewalk. Second, he "ordered" a subject to put a coin in an empty parking meter. Eighty-three percent of the people obeyed the security guard. Less than 50 percent obeyed the confederate in the other uniforms. The conclusion was that the security guard uniform added authority to the confederate, and the uniforms of others did not.

Other researchers have found that individuals tend to obey those who are dressed in a manner that demonstrates authority. As Bickman has noted, it may not be important whether that person actually has authority over the action being requested. For anyone who has interacted with a policewoman while speeding, the authority issue comes up but is rarely challenged. "Where have you been?" "When are you going?" These are at least irrelevant questions.

Once I was late getting to my office. There was only one parking space open in the lot. Right as I arrived, a person who appeared to be a student drove into the remaining parking space. I was in my suit with a tie. I motioned for him to leave the space so that I could take it. The student complied. Although it was a faculty space, I had no authority to make him move. But he moved, nonetheless.

To what extent will a person "follow" a person in authority? People waiting for a "don't cross" sign at a stop light stood there even though there was no oncoming traffic. When a suited individual violated the crosswalk signal first, however, others followed. If we see a policeman, we will not ask for any kind of authority support if he is wearing a uniform, even if he does not have a badge. If he is a plainclothes policeman, we may ask for evidence that he is a policeman.

The authority element has been noted clearly in the classic study undertaken by Stanley Milgram in *Obedience to Authority*. In the original study, Milgram (1974) advertised in newspapers for paid volunteers to participate in an experiment. When the subjects arrived, they were provided the scenario of how the experiment would take place. They met in twos. They were told that this was a learning task of matching words such as "blue box," "nice day," and "wild duck." The teacher would read the pairs of words. After listing several word pairs, the teacher asked the learner to answer multiple choice questions such as "blue: _____." If the learner answered correctly, the teacher moved on to the next pair of words. However, if the learner gave an incorrect answer, the teacher gave the person an electric shock.

To decide which subject would be the teacher, the experimenter said he would write down the words "teacher" and "learner" on two pieces of paper. Then each one took a piece of paper. The one who chose was the "outside" subject. The paper always said "teacher." When the two subjects heard the last part of the scenario, one of them stated that he had a heart problem, and that this might be a bad idea.

The experimenter assured him that although there might be a slight pain, there would be no long-lasting effects.

The learner (victim; confederate) was taken into a separate room, where the two could not see one another but the teacher could hear the learner. The victim was strapped into a chair with wires connected to him.

The experimenter showed the "teacher" a bank of switches that indicated how much electricity the learner would receive. There were thirty switches, ranging from fifteen volts to 450 volts. The list of word pairs was before the teacher. Once the learner missed a question, the teacher was supposed to give him the fifteen-volt shock. The severity of the shock increased with each incorrect question.

Once the shocks became too high, the learner yelled (it was actually an audio tape) that he couldn't take it anymore. Concern over inflicting pain and the fact that the learner had already stated that he had a health problem frequently caused the teacher to want to stop. The experimenter, seated behind the teacher, told the teacher to go on. The experimenter was dressed in a gray technician's coat. He took a stern approach with the learner.

The subjects were told in the beginning that they would be paid regardless of whether they finished the experiment.

Nevertheless, subjects who were reluctant to go on with the experiment asked about the money. They were assured they would be paid but were asked to continue. Many did continue. In fact, two-thirds punished the learner to the highest level of electrical shock.

The study was replicated decades later by the American Broadcasting Corporation (ABC). In their program, *Primetime,* the results were similar. Seventy-three percent of women and 65 percent of men complied with the experimenter's requests.

Actually, the learner was not shocked, but the subjects did not know that at the time.

Primetime also reported in a related story that a caller to a McDonald's restaurant telephoned saying that he was a policeman. He asked the assistant manager to call in a teenage girl employee to the office. When there, the caller asked that the manager to force the teenage employee to strip naked and perform jumping jacks. The authority in this case was simply a phone call with a voice that said he was a policeman. The manager complied. This event was repeated by the criminal who made the calls. An expanded version was shown in the movie, *Compliance*. If nothing else, these stories illustrate how easy it is to get someone to comply with almost any request, provided there is authority involved. It happened even in a request made over the telephone.

In another experiment, Philip Zimbardo (2007), a Stanford psychologist, randomly assigned a group of male college students to be guards and prisoners in a simulated prison. The "prisoners" complied with requests of the "guards" even though they knew that they had been randomly placed in their respective positions.

Subsequently, Zimbardo's and Milgram's studies were found to be unethical according to the American Psychological Association. The results of those studies and others such as the Tuskegee syphilis study provided the impetus for research to be more ethical. Of course, the McDonald's example was illegal, and the culprit was later imprisoned for the phone call and for others that he had made all over the country.

Of course, compliance can be used for good or evil or anywhere in between. But we know that compliance is much easier to achieve if the persuader engages his target with all of the nonverbal tools that increase credibility.

PHYSICAL APPEARANCE FOR BUSINESS SUCCESS

Given all these studies, the concept of authority, especially with uniforms, tends to increase one's ability to gain compliance from others. "Uniforms," as noted by Bickman, may be as simple as a tie and a suit.

Dressing for success depends on the particular occupation of the individual. But John T. Molloy (1988) has written much about clothing. His work indicates what men and women need to wear from head to toe to achieve success in white-collar businesses. In his first attempt at discovering success based on clothing, Molloy used a survey method to determine what the more socially and career-mobile businessperson wears. He began his studies simply looking at what color raincoats men wear to work. He found that there were two primary colors: beige (or tan) and black. He found that in higher-priced clothing stores more tan coats were sold, while at lower-priced stores more black raincoats were sold. Consequently, Molloy concluded that those in higher positions of authority in white-collar companies preferred tan.

His recommendations are quite specific. Even though his books were written in the late 1980s, most would appear to remain valid. In this context, though, please remember that he is talking about white-collar, corporate, and legal occupations.

MEN'S SUITS

Most importantly, Molloy indicates that men need to take more time shopping, especially in regard to suits. It is important to be in style, but with men's suits this is not necessarily a difficult task. They rarely change except for the width of the lapels and whether they are two-piece, three-piece, or double-breasted. Double-breasted suits rarely stay popular when they are popular, which is infrequently. The two piece is likely to be acceptable almost any time. The issue really becomes the fitting. For that reason, tailored suits are probably the best. In any case, fit is a primary criterion for the successful man's suit. One does not want a suit to fit too tightly nor to have wrinkles because of the size or the lack of pressing. It is important that the suit have a good feel to the wearer because that makes one more comfortable. The proper colors are gray, blue, and brown of varying shades. Solid suits and narrow pinstripes are the best. One should never mix the jackets and the trousers of different suits. Neither should the successful man wear a sports coat and slacks for business purposes.

One should not wear short-sleeved shirts for business. Any pocket monograms should be small and discreet. Molloy goes on to explain that solid shirts and a few stripes are acceptable. Any other pattern is unacceptable.

Ties may be the most important part of a man's wardrobe. I recall my children giving me a Sponge Bob Square Pants tie, but I have not worn it to work (to their chagrin). Molloy suggests that one should not get assistance with this task from secretaries, wives, girlfriends, or even clerks at a clothing store. The first concern is the length of the tie. It should fall to the belt. The width of the tie is important as well. The popularity of tie widths varies from time to time. Basically, the width should match the width of suit lapels. One should be careful about patterns as well. Sponge Bob is not the only bad tie. One should watch for ties that associate them with politics, religions, and other organizations. There should be no large images. The Ivy League striped tie or a solid tie is best.

Business socks should be solid colors and dark. Although at times there is a popularity of yellow socks or socks with designs, they are not for business. Even in business contexts, though, there are sometimes fads in socks. Molloy's recommended shoe is the wingtip. Black should be worn with gray, blue, or black suits and brown with brown. They should not be droopy. They should be worn over the calf. Again, there are slight changes from time to time, but for business there should be no flip flops, sandals, loafers, or boots. Most now consider wingtips as highly formal.

Tie pins are out of date. Lapel pins usually should not be worn, especially if they indicate some political or religious undertones. The same is true for class rings. If the other person needs to know where you went to college, they probably already do. Bracelets are a no-no. Cuff links should be small and simple, and they should not be identified with any kind of organization. A man should not wear any chains or necklaces or earrings, according to Molloy. The only acceptable ring is a wedding ring. The only other piece of jewelry that is acceptable is a simple watch.

In general terms, one does not want to appear to be a cowboy with a huge belt buckle of a rodeo guy herding a calf (unless maybe you are in Texas). One should not appear like someone from a criminal organization in the 1930s. Do not appear in any way any less than you are. These simple rules will assist your credibility at work and will help gain compliance from others anywhere.

WOMEN'S DRESS FOR SUCCESS

Molloy (1996) has also written about success through dress for women. There are some minor differences between menswear and women's clothing, but for the most part they are similar. To begin, though, I should note that neither dresses nor sweaters are appropriate for women in the workplace.

Some years ago, decades ago, I was presenting the information in this chapter of Molloy's book to a couple of hundred women who taught home economics in Mississippi high schools. Some also taught in college. I had my notes, and I was about to state what color suits not to wear in business. I looked out into the audience (thankfully) before I spoke. I saw purple, pink, yellow, and lime suits out there. I quickly moved to my next point before talking about the color of suits for business success. Of course, these teachers were teachers, not business executives. I avoided the topic anyway.

According to Molloy, the lowest popularity for the women's suit was in 1989. In his first edition of the women's manual for business success, Molloy had advocated almost exclusively the skirted suit. But since its lowest popularity, the pantsuit has become almost, if not more popular, than the skirted suit. Two of the worst errors that women make with their outfits are that they try to appear too masculine, sometimes even wearing a tie, or they maintain the fashion values they had growing up. In the latter case, they had a lower position and less money. They may have been unwilling to pay a substantial sum for clothing.

Women have credibility with medium-blue and navy-blue suits with a white blouse. Others that rated high were beige with some gray, tan, and camel. Blue, gray, and beige are the colors that one should keep in mind. The pants should be full fit. Women should remember that they are not dressing for a potential date but for credibility in business. Women in executive positions should not wear sweaters. They were tested as clothing that a lower-level clerical person might wear.

A woman should take care with blouses. They should not be too frilly. The neckline should not be too low. Scarves should be used to cover up the neckline if there is any doubt about the neckline. White and pastel blouses are generally acceptable. In order, the most recommended are pale blue, white, light beige, beige with hint of gray, rust, pale yellow, maroon, red, and ecru. The only place where patterns should appear is with scarves. Solid, plaid, paisley, stripe, and polka dots are acceptable. Molloy recommended pumps for dressing for success. The colors include navy, medium, blue, black, deep brown, maroon, beige, cordovan, and tan. Notice that high heels are not recommended, nor are red shoes for business. Flesh-colored hose are recommended. Certainly, a woman should not wear fishnet stockings, and should not wear white (unless perhaps she is a nurse).

For business purposes, women should not dress as if they are going out. They should dress for the status they intend to have. They may need to forget their socioeconomic history. A wardrobe should be considered a business investment. I don't know whether the Internal Revenue Service would agree that the wardrobe is a business expense, but perhaps it should be. One final notion. Molloy wrote that a jacket that is not part of a suit should be part of the wardrobe. The preferred colors include black, white, dark gray, medium blue, light blue, light gray, medium gray dark brown, medium brown, green, maroon and rust.

As with men, women should dress for the position they are seeking. Believe it or not, executives of both sexes notice how one looks. Certainly, if they are hiring someone to interact with other executives, they want them to look the part.

Most importantly, one should be fully dressed before leaving the greenroom. Make sure that all buttons are buttoned, and all zippers are zipped. Make sure the shirt or blouse tails are tucked in properly. Be sure that all the clothing is in alignment. For men, make sure the tie is properly tied and that it does not show behind the collar. Check, check, check.

In the business world, wearing costumes like those suggested by Molloy is a first step in acting the part. We all know that what we wear is not only what others see but also for our self-perception. We also know that costumes are for particular scenes and particular acts. When we see a man at a children's soccer match wearing coat and tie, we do assess his costume. Either he didn't have time to go home and change, he has another meeting later, or he is trying to impress people who are less than impressed.

ARTIFACTS (PROPS)

Several researchers have used the term "artifacts" to refer to basic items that we carry with us. Using Goffman's analogy to theater, they can be called props. Many of these remain what they were decades ago, and others change with the times. Years ago, the science and math types used to carry slide rules with them. The slide rules had cases, and the mathematical rule was connected to the belt of the engineering major. They were replaced by calculators. Since phones have calculators, many calculators have been replaced by phones.

Almost everyone carries a wallet of some sort. In today's world, one must have a case for credit cards, money, and driver's license. Men typically carry theirs in the pants pocket, and women usually have theirs in a purse. Men frequently do not understand why women have so many things in their purses. Under ordinary circumstances, a wallet is not large enough to hold the various artifacts that one needs to carry. Because of the lack of space, women typically turn to purses, and men turn to briefcases. But men have an advantage in their clothing, also. Men's pockets are made to hold various items. There are front and back pants pockets, shirt pockets, and usually at least four coat pockets. Men place watches, cell phones, keys, combs, smoking artifacts, as well as folded papers, passports, and glasses in their pockets. For women, most of these items are relegated to the purse. This fact presents women with the disadvantage that they must carry something with them.

Businesswomen may use a brief case instead of a purse. In business situations, it places the men and women on equal status and typically no one knows what is in anyone else's briefcase. These days, an iPad or laptop may be part of the items in the briefcase. These electronic devices allow one to eliminate many of the papers they previously stored in a carrying case.

Of course, the number one artifact in today's world is the smartphone. It seems almost everyone has one, and a people who don't are considered an artifact or a relic themselves. Such mobile communication devices have been around for some time. The car phone was one of those movie props in some films including those with James Bond. Beepers became the devices for emergency medical personnel and drug dealers in the 1980s. Now cellular telephones have become the best and the worst for communication. The "smart watch" has become popular as well. I recall the smart watch as a significant device in the Dick Tracy comic strip in the 1950s. Eventually technology catches up with art.

Of all these devices, though, the smartphone has created the most problems as well as the most solutions. Texting on a cellular phone has become such a driving distraction that most locales have made the practice

WHY ARE YOU TELLING ME THIS?

illegal. Unfortunately, such a law is difficult to enforce because most laws do not make talking on the phone illegal. These phones have also become addictions of sorts. Each semester I have a policy in my course syllabi that students may not use these phones in class. Each semester I have violations by several students. Even if I tell them they will be dismissed from the class or lose points, they cannot tear themselves away. What the smartphone has become is a virtual added limb.

Of course, there are students who abide by the policy. Even those, though, want to have their phones in sight. The interesting thing to me is that I have taught in college for over fifty years, and I have never had a student receive an emergency call. Never. I have to wonder whether there are more emergencies today or whether students are addicted.

In my discussions with students, there are both legitimate and illegitimate uses of electronic devices in the classroom. I had one graduate student who would check the accuracy of what I was saying. I see that to be legitimate. Somewhat threatening, but legitimate. Others, most of them, check their tweets and check their text messages. In some ways this is no different from people who used to arrive at home and immediately check their emails and phone messages. In other ways, though, the cell phone is a constant.

I wondered why all of this was necessary. After discussing this with several students in several classes, I have come to two conclusions about addicted cell phone users. Many are either lonely or bored or both. This is not to say that most phone users are addicts. In fact, most are not. Even though I have one or two in class each year, that is just one or two out of a couple of hundred.

There are other professors who become more irritated than I do about cell phones. I try to create analogies for current behavior in the classroom versus, say, forty years ago. I remember as a student, I doodled a lot. My class notes were about half notes and half doodles. As we all know, there are few professors who are interesting every minute. Professors get off track, we are thrown off track, we are redundant. These are triggers for doodling or texting, I guess. Many do not doodle today because they do not carry pens or pencils with them. The phone and the laptop and the electronic pad have replaced paper and pencil. They are, though, artifacts.

IN THE MIRROR

Most of us would like others to think that our looking in a mirror is a rare occasion. The fact is, though, that we do look. At least when we prepare for the day in the morning, men brush their teeth, brush or comb their hair, shave their faces, apply deodorant, check to see if they need to eliminate unwanted hair in their ears or around their eyes, adjust their ties, and check for any cuts made while shaving. Women brush their teeth, apply makeup, apply lipstick, brush or comb their hair, apply deodorant, adjust their blouses, and double-check everything.

But looking in the mirror in the morning is just the first time for both sexes. When men and women go to the restroom at any time of day, they wash their hands, and, yes, take another look into the mirror. Over the course of the day, cosmetics can become distorted because of the weather and because of bodily conditions such as perspiration. Thus, some cosmetics must be reapplied. Reapplying lipstick, for example, may take place several times per day.

The mirror is used for an assessment and for corrections. The assessment is a means of comparing one's physical concept of self with that of other people. Elaine Berscheid and her colleagues underscored the importance of self-assessment in a study of body image.

Gender	Slightly Dissatisfied	Extremely Satisfied
Female	23%	45%
Male	15%	55%

Table 1.
Overall Body Satisfaction by Sex.
Taken from Berscheid et al. (1973)

Although their study was conducted in 1973, there is little reason to believe that we have changed much about how we perceive ourselves. Other studies in the 1980s basically confirmed the previous study. Bersheid and her colleagues found that men were most dissatisfied with their abdomen (47 percent) and buttocks (26 percent) while women were dissatisfied with their hips (71 percent), their abdomen (69 percent), and buttocks (60 percent).

In the facial area, the most dissatisfaction was with the teeth. Although the teeth remain a significant concern, we have seen recently that women have a concern about the size of their lips. Injections have become quite popular. In addition, there has historically been a major concern with the nose, and plastic surgery has been used to change the shape, frequently to make the nose smaller. Of course, liposuction has become a quick fix to being overweight, and it is much more efficient than diets and exercise.

The question becomes, "Why are people doing these things?" For the most part there are two reasons: (1) to appear younger and (2) to increase sex appeal. Berscheid and her colleagues (1973) had one rather interesting conclusion. The subjects who had engaged in sexual relations with more than ten others during their lifetimes had a better image than those who had had sex with fewer than ten others. Though the researchers did not go into "why" questions, one must wonder if those who had engaged in more sexual relationships were more satisfied because they had engaged so much or whether they engaged in sex so much because they were more satisfied. Perhaps some explanations can be found in how the data were collected.

The body image survey was included in a popular magazine, *Psychology Today*, as an insert. The respondents completed the survey and returned it. Obviously, these were readers of the magazine, either by subscription or individual purchases. The readers were mostly between the ages of eighteen and fifty. One should also remember that 1973 was during the period of the sexual revolution. Even so, the study supports the notion that body image is closely associated with sexual relationships. More than 60,000 people were apparently interested in the topic because they completed and mailed the survey back to the researchers.

Two other conclusions were interesting. First, as women grew older, their perceptions of their bodies were that they became more dissatisfied. Men, though, had more satisfaction with their bodies as they grew older. Second, there were questions about "sexual parts" of men and women based on what was traditionally considered sexual. One in four women were concerned about breast size. Fifteen percent of men were concerned about their penis size. The American Society of Aesthetic Plastic Surgery reported in 2011 that there had been nearly 9.5 million surgical and nonsurgical changes in patients' bodies during the previous year. Of the over 1.6 million changes by surgery, more than 500,000 involved breast surgery to correct too much, too little, and the wrong shape. Liposuction, facelifts, and rhinoplasty were performed more than 120,000 times each.

The rate of breast surgery certainly indicates that women still consider their breast size to be important. Although most men do not have surgery, they use a variety of means to try to increase their penis size. As things change, many remain the same. And men's desire to present a sexual image has become even larger with the variety of erectile dysfunction pills.

APPEARANCE AND CREDIBILITY

Two of my colleagues and I were interested in how minor factors influence one's credibility. We studied hair color, eye color, eyeglasses, and smoking artifacts. The smoking artifacts question may lend some background for how these studies took place. My colleagues and I were talking in the office one day, and we all knew we were right about smoking. Two of us smoked a pipe, and the third is a nonsmoker.

We were not right about the smoking itself. The argument was more about smoking and credibility. We started out arguing about whether a pipe smoker or a nonsmoker is more credible. Then we decided to test the issue using human subjects. We also included cigars and cigarettes in our analysis. None of us thought that cigars or cigarettes added to one's credibility, though.

Our conclusions were pretty much what one would expect. The nonsmoker and the pipe smoker were considered more credible than the cigar smoker. The cigarette was so low that one might consider it negative credibility. Ten years later, we found that smoking in general is not credible.

In the hair color study, we had subjects rate the same woman's photograph with the same hairstyle but with blond, brunette, and red hair. There were no differences in credibility. The same was true of eyeglasses. Various styles of glasses produced no differences. Perhaps this is because we know that some others wear contacts. That is not to say that some people intentionally use a style of glasses to make themselves appear more "nerdy." In our world today, though, wearing glasses does not mean that you are any more of an intellect than those who do not. Eye color was a different situation. We had two different pictures of the same woman as subjects to rate. The pictures were the same except that the woman had blue eyes in one case and brown eyes in the other. The respondents indicated that they preferred the blue-eyed woman for social relationships, but they preferred the brown-eyed picture for working relationships. Such a conclusion may not be obvious from intuition. In fact, most of us are rarely consciously aware of eye color.

STIGMAS

A former student of mine told me this story about a friend who walked him to the library. The former student is blind, and he walked with a cane. In special situations, a friend walked along with him. In this case, they were going to the university library to check out some books in braille. The two of them walked to a librarian's desk, and her question was: "What does he want?" My student was standing right there. I suppose by asking the other student, she did not have to yell. The point is that people who have a stigma are evaluated as if they have numerous stigmas. Thus, from the librarian's viewpoint, the blind student apparently could not hear well.

We engage in such behavior with others who may have no stigma at all. If a person with an accent that is not American or not English asks for directions, we might respond loudly and point. Foreigners may have a certain stigma about them even though they should not be stigmatized. We may also respond more slowly—which may or may not be a good idea. Having visited countries where Thai, Japanese, Portuguese, Spanish, and German are spoken, I would be one of those stigmatized people in their country. I never noticed their engaging in such negative behaviors, though.

A study was undertaken in California in which a person posed in a wheelchair with a rubber hose hanging from her nose. In the other condition, she had no stigma. In both cases, she asked passersby at an airport for directions to a certain city. When she was in the wheelchair, those responding to her stood further away, talked more slowly, and took more time explaining directions.

STATUS AND CLOTHING

In today's world, if someone is rich enough, she can obviously wear whatever she wants. It's somewhat interesting how counterculture idiosyncrasies later became status symbols. For example, if one had a hole in his blue jeans (and they were all blue) in the 1950s and 1960s, she purchased "patches" that were ironed on to the jeans to cover up the holes. In the twenty-first century, teenagers purchase jeans with holes already in them. Guys with long hair in the '70s were usually considered part of the hippie generation, and they were perceived to be liberal—anti-war, pro-choice, women's advocates, and civil rights protesters. But later, farm boys and blue-collar men began wearing long hair, and it was assumed they drove a pickup truck with a shotgun and a Confederate flag as accessories.

When analyzing what a person has chosen to wear, we need to be careful that we understand they are merely trying to present an image. Once we know and understand that we can move on the image and to what extent the image is truly part of who they are. Thus, the three-piece suit does not always mean high status. In fact, the most high-status persons, like Bill Gates and Warren Buffett, probably do not care about their image because everyone knows who they are.

OVERVIEW

We prepare for human interaction in a similar manner as we would to go on stage. We have makeup and costumes for different occasions. We spend a lot of money and spend a lot of time doing this. Perhaps the hope is that we will be the star of the show. The other actors do the same, and they critique us as the play goes on. We do the same with them. In many cases, we try to be ourselves. Unfortunately, we may not know who that is, and we may truly be different people at different times.

CHAPTER 6

THE ONE ABOUT THE DISK JOCKEY: TRICKY VOICES IN THE WORLD

When I was sixteen, I was a disk jockey at a radio station. This was pre-iPod, predigital, and long before Beyonce and Lady Gaga, but not preradio. This was way back when music meant vinyl records played on turntables, and songs were delivered to listeners via airwaves. At the one-kilowatt station where I worked, I played top-forty music; read the news, weather, and sports; and played previously recorded commercials. On occasion, I was allowed to read advertisements "live."

I had no breaks except when a song played. In general, these forty-five-rpm recordings lasted less than three minutes. My weekend hours were from 6 a.m. until 5:30 p.m. When I read the hog market report at the beginning of the day and when I read the sign-off statement at sundown, the listeners expected me to sound equally as enthusiastic. If the radio disk jockey sounded depressed at 6 a.m. or tired at 5:30 p.m., the audience thought the radio personality was not very good at the job. They expected the performance to stay even, balanced, and fresh, never letting on that there is a real person of flesh and blood behind the voice. If the disk jockey did it right, he learned to "fake" feeling fresh no matter what his real feelings were at the time. These are a few of the reasons that many contemporary radio stations today are "automated." In essence, a computer is the disk jockey.

This is true of other types of performances as well. Think of the TV reporter who drops his cool facade. Believing the camera is no longer "live," he throws his notepad down in frustration at some flub he made on air. His temper tantrum catches the attention of the internet viewer and goes viral. After this clip receives numerous hits and refuses to die, the reporter resigns. Presumably his audience no longer sees him as cool, calm, and collected as he delivers the news. The real problem is he's too much like the rest of us. Most of us have been known to lose our temper when something doesn't go right. But YouTube never lets the audience forget the unforgiveable transgression of being human and forgetting to practice the performer's deception. These behaviors are quite commonly reported about sports coaches on social media.

It was largely through my radio experience that I learned how to practice deception in life. As a disk jockey, I tried to change my voice, intending to sound a little less southern and a lot older. I adapted a radio "personality" or pseudonym as well. I wanted neither the regular adult listeners nor my high school classmates to realize that Dick Jones, the disk jockey, was actually Mark. In retrospect, I think even I sometimes thought of Dick and Mark as separate people!

One high school female student, who was a habitual caller to the station, phoned to ask if I were really her classmate. I knew who she was, but, until I confirmed it, apparently she did not know my identity. Even though I answered her question honestly, she remained a true nonbeliever. Toward that end, she came to the radio station. I saw her studying me through the lobby window just outside of the control room where I worked. Even then, she still contended that I was not Mark, her classmate. At a break, I showed her my driver's license. Faced with the documentation, she burst into tears and quickly left. I never knew if her emotional response was because she liked her fantasy about the deceptive voice I used, or because she disliked the real teenage me, or because she was embarrassed about being fooled. In any case, she never called me at the radio station again.

Because of my deepened voice, I am certain the audience perceived me as a much more mature person than I was. That was true in part, too, because they were dependent on me to some degree for the weather and news, as well as the football scores.

Frequently in classes that I teach, a student will request that I repeat something that I have said. I usually respond by asking her a question, which is: "Do you want me to repeat it exactly? Or do you want me to say it in different words? The reason I ask that is that the student sometimes wants me to repeat what I said and at other times she wants me to say what

I meant. The distinction is important for several reasons. First, the student may not have heard it. At my age, I know many people who cannot hear well. Certainly, if there are other noises around, it is frequently impossible to hear. Other distractions, too, such as computers and cell phones have the same effect. Third, there are vocal characteristics that also may affect what I say.

Vocalics is that aspect of nonverbal communication that deals with how we say the words that we say. Vocalics does not include the words per se. That aspect is considered in the chapter on words. In the simple three-word sentence, "I love you," there are at least three possible meanings depending on which of the three is emphasized.

There is "I *love* you." This sentence distinguishes between liking and loving, among other things. The sentence "*I* love you" illustrates the notion that regardless of what other people may think, my feelings are obvious. Frequently, such a sentence is stated when the other feels unloved in general. The third sentence, "I love *you*," signifies that the other is the target of the sentence. Regardless of whomever else I may love, I definitely love you. This is also the response to someone who has just said that they feel that way toward you.

Acoustic violations have been previously discussed as well.

Another interesting violation can be conducted by the speaker himself. For lack of a better term, I am calling it "underlying snicker." This vocal phenomenon occurs when a person either ends a message with a brief ha ha, or when they ha ha throughout their message. When they do, it sounds as if they are not serious about what they are saying. Most people do this on occasion. Others do it habitually. The underlying snicker is not intended to be sarcastic as may be the case with a snicker. Laughter is a sound that is part of vocalics.

We rarely think about it, but there are different types of laughs. The type of laughter a person has can influence their credibility. Laughter can be a howl, a screaming laugh, a giggle, a snort, a chuckle, a chortle, a howl, a roar, and others. A loud laugh is generally perceived as negative, and some people can be recognized by their laugh alone.

Moore, Hickson, and Stacks (2014) have identified several other identification cues that appear available through vocalics. One consideration about such identification that was not traditionally considered is the faux voice. Automated computers have taken over much of what we think of as customer service. They make telemarketing calls, and they guide us through trees of extensions that we may want to contact. Most of us can tell when a robot call occurs. It appears although some of them get close to sounding like a person, they just do not.

One characteristic to listen for in a person's voice is the accent. For the most part, we can determine whether another person's accent is the same as ours. We are more often capable to hear an accent if the other person is not a native English speaker. We have learned, though, that it would be a mistake to attach low credibility to them. We can also tell if some speakers are not native to the geographic area that we are from. Middle American accents are the most credible. In some sense, we use another person's accent as a supplement to the question, "Where are you from?" Some of us associate poor grammar with a geographical accent, whether it is southern or rural. Again, vocalics are not usually related to expertise in language.

VOCALICS AND GENDER DIFFERENCES

Deborah Tannen has written extensively about gender differences in vocalics. Here we will briefly discuss a few of these factors. For one, the concept of catharsis is apparently used and understood less by those of the masculine gender. When a person is simply trying to "blow off steam," a large percentage of males will answer by trying to solve the problem. I would add here that males tend to use persuasion more and communication less.

Persuasion is an attempt to get another person to change an attitude or behavior. Communication is an attempt to provide information to the other person. Remember catharsis is saying something to yourself even if others are present. Vocalics affects all three of the purposes of interaction.

An excellent video, "It's Not About the Nail," explains catharsis. In it, a man and a woman are talking. She is trying to use catharsis, but he insists on trying to solve her problem. The research on who talks more, men or women, is somewhat complicated. Men tend to talk more in public, and women talk more in private. However, women tend to provide more details in their conversations.

The genders tend to differ about interrupting as well. Most of the time men argue to try to get their point across and may interrupt to do so. Women interrupt to indicate their agreement with the other person. A seemingly irrelevant interruption, such as "Please pass the peas" during a dinner conversation about the politics of the day, is a neutral interruption.

Most people allow an interruption to go ahead. Others stop the interrupter immediately and may discuss the rudeness of the interruption. On television, some debaters try to talk over one another, and the two make the conversation meaningless for viewers because they can hear neither one.

Another viewpoint is when the person is interrupted even though she is not talking. This occurs when a person is trying to concentrate on doing something. The interrupter comes into the room and starts a conversation about a topic irrelevant to the mission of the first party. Frequently, this ends up causing a temper tantrum by the first party, going beyond calling the interrupter rude.

VOCAL DIFFICULTIES

A few "errors" that occur in vocalics are stuttering, separating parts of a sentence with "ah," and other types of filled pauses. Stuttering can be caused by several factors, but it is generally correctable. When a person stutters rarely, it is probably caused by nervousness. The "ah" and filled pauses, "like, you know" may be caused by some nervous tension and the lack of organizing what one is going to say before you say it. Some of these separations are natural. If you watch a movie or television program, there is rarely such a pause, but that seems unrealistic. Stuttering can usually be corrected, although even after a person who has had therapy for it, they may "slip" every now and then. It should not be mocked by the other person.

Another question that we may ask is why some people talk so loudly. We know that people with hearing difficulty talk loudly or very softly. Because they have problems hearing, they are often unable to know how loud they are talking. Others want to be heard. They speak loudly almost all the time. That was the case with the man who attended the speech and wanted everyone to know he was there. Loud accompanies big gestures and the desire for attention. It also makes the speaker sound more authoritative. Another reason may be that the person comes from a large family where loudness was the only way to be heard.

What might be considered violent speech is often accompanied by curse words. Violent speech is loud. We need to be able to distinguish among people who are loud so their parents can hear them, people being loud to show authority or persuasiveness, and those who are articulating verbal violence. The most significant part of verbal violence is whether it occurs frequently. It could be the beginning of a serious problem.

OVERVIEW

The sounds that we make through our voices are significant for how people view us. They can range from the "angel" voices that children use to sing at church presentations to the yelling a football coach does at a game. While most of us do not think about our voices much, we need to recognize that it says something about us. Many of us create a "new voice" as I did for radio. The radio situation illustrates that others have a vision of you based solely on the voice. These sounds tell others where you are from, maybe what you do (or don't do), what's important to you, to some extent your socioeconomic status, and your ability to communicate.

CHAPTER 7

IN THE BEGINNING WAS THE WORD

Aside from how we say the words we say, the words themselves appear to have different values to different people. As Addeo and Burger (1974) wrote fifty years ago, we appear to have contexts in which we begin to use words that are appropriate for the environment. This notion they referred to as "ego speak." Here we will discuss one or two of Addeo and Burger's concepts and add a few of our own. Generally, we think of specialized language coming from physicians, lawyers, engineers, and other professionals. However, almost all of us engage in some sort of specialized language at work. It seems that it is important to let the nonspecialists know they are ignorant to our specialized knowledge and vocabulary.

TYPES OF TALK

Among those ego-speak roles that Addeo and Burger (1974, 20–15) discuss is *job speak/business speak*. We have already discussed how specialized language is used to show people how much more we know that others. An additional aspect of job speak is that of talking *about* a job to a spouse or colleague. It may be that the person is trying to show some power that they may or may not have had. For example, "I told our boss yesterday we needed to do things differently." The reason for doing this has little to do with changing things and more about "I *told* our boss." In all likelihood, that conversation when the guy told off his boss never happened. I have previously analyzed this type of conversation among masculine interactants (Hickson 2013). Another way of showing power or contacts is name-dropping. "I just saw Tom Hanks at the airport" is an example. The talker hasn't even met the person. Or someone will say they "heard" that a friend saw an important person. Name-dropping is not as common among those who truly have power.

The concept of *"taking charge" talk* is interpreted differently by masculine receivers. Two types, the military and the nurturer, do not seem like the same but are quite similar. When a parent says, "You *need* to take a coat," a child may interpret that as "You *must* take a coat." These messages may or may not always be gender related. However, Tannen (1990) suggested that feminine communicators are more likely to be nurturers, and male communicators are more likely to be controllers.

Taking charge or authoritative talk is related to what transactional psychologists call the parent role (Berne 1964). The parent must tell the children what to do and what not to do. Sometimes the parents explain why they say something. Many times, the response is simply "because I said so." This is not a satisfactory response, but it is a frequent response. The parent is saying, "I am the authority and you are not." The opposite is a child's talk, much of which is making excuses.

Academic talk is one of those specialties where people try to prove how smart they are. In academia, though, academics of different subjects may have different vocabulary words. Many academics *always* talk that way. It is also true that some people who are not academics try to talk like academics. When another person uses academic talk, it frequently comes across as a lecture.

When is person completes the dissertation (thesis) for a PhD, the student must have an oral examination on their final submission. Several people on the committee ask questions of the student. When I had my examination, the department chair, who I am convinced to this day never read my thesis, asked me: "Are there some simpler words you could use in parts of the dissertation?" I was literally defenseless when I asked for an example. He picked out: "empirically grounded model." I responded saying that my professor and I had first chosen "emergent, isomorphic paradigm." My critic did not ask another question. I had not intended it as a smart-ass answer, although I am certain it sounded that way. The fact is he was right. An "observation model" should have been good enough.

But a dissertation is an academic paper, and academics must sometimes show that they are academics.

Closely related to academic talk is *sophisticated talk*. Here the talkers are more concerned about how sophisticated they may sound. They must be "up to snuff" on the community and the world. They should keep up with the *New York Times* best sellers list, should have read most of the books on the list, and should have an acceptable opinion of them. Some esoteric comparison of one of the books with one of the classics adds to their credibility. The same is true of the current playlist on Broadway. Sophisticates know how to talk this way. They don't use contractions and make certain they are extremely articulate. Some can also translate to a less sophisticated person or change topics for them. Sophisticates also know what not to talk about. They do not curse in public or in places where the opposite gender is present.

Another version of sophisticated talk is *bureaucratic talk*. This is a specialized language as much as some of the others are. Instead of showing knowledge about the specialty, these people use acronyms to show their experience and tenure. A new member of such a business group often cannot tell what is going on in the meeting with BLM, CIA, USPS and shortened names for what they are discussing.

Sales talk is something we encounter often. When the salesperson meets the potential customer, he repeatedly says the customer's name. "Well, Mark, you have a whole new line this year. Mark, you have a special opportunity to get yours today." They "Mark" you to death. They tend to rush you into making a decision, always suggesting that there is a limited time for you to get the deal. In some sense, they probably repeat your name so that they can remember it. In another sense, the person using sales talk may think that saying your name makes the two of you seem closer. They may ask about your family and your job to "get to know you," but the truth is they are simply trying to make a sale. In complex organizations, there are training sessions to remind you to repeat the customer's name.

Politically correct talk begins with politicians themselves. The goal of politicians is to talk in a manner that is ambiguous enough that they can get as many votes as possible. They must say things that appeal to their base constituency. Often the politician wraps the pro-party talk with words that won't offend the opponent's constituency. Historically, the politician attempted to obtain voters from all segments of the population. In interviews with the media, the candidate might be asked, "What is the answer to the budget problem?" Then the politician answers with something like, "We have been working on the budget problem for some time now. There have been some good points on all sides of the issue. I think we will work it out soon." In other words, she does not answer the question. Answers were not to offend anyone.

That approach has been taken up by nonprofessionals. The idea among nonprofessionals is that you should not say anything to hurt anybody's feelings. The approach says that you should not denigrate a person by putting them in a negative category. You should not negatively evaluate groups. You need to be careful about words because those words might be interpreted as negative. Especially offensive are words related to culture, gender, or race. Political correctness in language causes many to self-censor.

Sex talk tends to fly in the face of politically correct talk. In the beginning, this talk may be considered flirtatious. Flirting is just the starting point. A person may refer to body parts in some ambiguous fashion, which turns into more sexy terms for the same body part. The target may go along with it or push it away. When it becomes habitual and the resistance has been habitual, it may become inappropriate and even illegal.

Religious talk might include certain topics of conversation. It also includes certain words that most people don't use in everyday conversation. The word "blessed," is used frequently. This is the religious substitute for "lucky" or "fortunate." It has a different meaning for the sender, but nonreligious people would consider them synonyms.

There are times when we can determine much about another person with just a one-word substitution. Does he say "we" as much as "I"? How much of the conversation is about the other person? How much does one person dominate the conversation? When can we tell? The better communicator will probably use "you" or "we" more often than "I."

I was at a bar in Atlanta where there was a group of strangers. In all fairness, it seemed like they had been drinking for some time. They were dressed in such a manner that appeared to me that they were having an after-party following a wedding reception. They held conversation about money. One of them said money was not important to him. He went on for about thirty minutes about how money was not important. I surmised that he thought money *was* important. The traditional saying for this is, "You protest too much." There are times when a person says the opposite of what they mean.

The types of talk we have discussed seem to indicate that the purpose is to show some power differential (I know more than you. I am more experienced than you. I am your boss. I am your superior). Otherwise, they are roles to obtain something. The kinds of talk that we engage are somewhat natural to each of us, but some of them also come from workshops or experience. With all these types of talk it is not surprising that it is difficult for any of us to be authentic and almost as hard to determine who the authentic "me" is.

Authenticity is difficult to define, but here is my take on it. An authentic person is one who believes that he or she is talking in a spontaneous way, with little or no planning involved. That is, authentic means that the person must believe in themselves and not be fake or phony. The authentic person is the opposite of what political handlers offer their candidates.

This list types of talk is not a complete one. There certainly may be more. None of the categories is mutually exclusive. For example, a minister may have a religious talk and a sales talk. The religious talk may encompass most of their sermons, but when it comes to the church budget they shift into sales talk and business talk. Additionally, each type of talk has degrees of intensity. Sales talk from your alumni association may not be as "hard sell" as the talk from a car dealer.

WORDS THAT SEEM TO MAKE SENSE, BUT DON'T

I often heard meteorologists around the country use "actually" in a ridiculous way. The whole country hung on to that word for about five years. The weather person would say something like, "It's actually fifty-five degrees." There is little wrong with it, but it is irritating. It's unnecessary. What other kinds of fifty-five degrees are there?

"Flustrated," a word that does not exist, does fulfill a legitimate purpose. It is a combination of flustered and frustrated. Mr. Webster should consider putting it in the book.

Another word that does exist but is used improperly more often that it is used properly is "literally." I have heard various versions of something that literally happened. The most significant to me was "It literally killed me." I had doubts about that.

INTENTIONAL MISUSE OF WORDS

I don't know if there is a course at some university on the misuse of words in which the end goal is to teach people to use words inappropriately, but I think at times that there must be. Politicians and political parties intentionally misuse words for persuasion purposes. At times, advertising and marketing do the same. In interpersonal communication the tactic of misusing words is most often used when an individual is trying to hide the truth of some action.

Communication scholars have argued for decades, if not centuries, how important words are and what they mean to us. Some thought that words are important. Certainly, a politically correct talker would think that. Those on that side of the argument would suggest that "we are what we say." Perhaps this is one of the reasons that "bad guys" as portrayed in films are the people who curse. To some extent, the concept that we are what we say has some problems. First, we do not always know exactly what words to use, or we cannot think of them in the moment. This is one of the reasons that we find ourselves apologizing later for something we said previously.

THE WORD IS NOT THE THING

One viewpoint is that words are merely symbols for actual persons, things, or events. This viewpoint is referred to as general semantics (Korzybski 2010). The author of this approach, Alfred Korzybski, was a Polish physicist who wanted to clarify language to make it more logical and better to be representative of "reality." Much of his work was to correct notions that had been made by Aristotle centuries earlier. A simple example is what is called the fallacy of "either/or." We frequently use language this way.

When I was in a restaurant in Illinois, a waitress asked me whether I wanted mustard *or* ketchup for my hamburger. I answered, "Both." In retrospect, I am not sure that she intended me to choose one or the other. I could have. I also could have answered, "Neither." Whereas Aristotle would have intended for me to choose one or the other, a general semanticist would suggest that a forced either/or does not account for all of the possibilities. It is common that we phrase questions in either/or terms, even though we know that there can frequently be neither/both as well as either/or. The either/or phenomenon is common even in our digital age.

When general semanticists argue that "the word is not the thing," they mean that a word is a metaphor for a thing. We know this because if we write a word, such as "weed" on a board, we know that we can neither smoke it nor pull it from the ground. General semantics theory supports the notion of "sticks and stones can break my bones but words will never hurt me." Realistically, we know that sometimes words do hurt us, even if they shouldn't. There are some people who must encounter words intended to hurt them often. Just recently, several professional basketball players admitted they had to learn to "unhear" what fans at opposing venues were yelling at them. When a person attacks you, it may be a good idea to take the advice of NBA players.

General semantics is based on "the word is not the thing," but in addition there are several suggestions that its advocates recommend. An understanding of general semantics requires us to take a look at the bases of the concept. Words and ideas are considered internal or external. I can have an idea of food in my mind (internal) but that is different from seeing, smelling, or tasting food that is present (external). In addition, this approach provides recommendations for making our personal language more consistent with the external "reality."

INTERNAL VERSUS EXTERNAL

Stacks, Hill, and Hickson (1991) illustrate some reasons why people do not use language well.

The first is that we pay more attention to what we call something than we do to the things themselves. For example, a hamburger restaurant wanted to get more business for its milkshakes, even though society was pushing for us to lose weight. The restaurant chain created the Skinny Shake. Its sales increased and the buyers felt good about themselves, but the ingredients in the shake were the same. They just called it a Skinny Shake. Second, people respond to words as if they were real things. Many do not like to hear the word "snake." Some react as if there were a real snake there. Third, people do not respond to "facts" even if they know they are facts. For example, we know that smoking cigarettes is bad for us. Some people smoke anyway. They may give excuses or they may simply admit that they have an addiction. Most of us agree that wearing a seat belt is a good idea. Some people do not do it anyway. The list of admonitions that we are aware of but that we do not follow can be long. Being overweight is another. Finally, we sometimes use verbal proofs to illustrate something when those proofs are meaningless. For example, in the college football context, loyal fans bet on their teams based on this illogic. "If Notre Dame beat Michigan, and Michigan beat Ohio State, then Notre Dame will beat Ohio State." The primary reason this does not work is that "teams" do not remain the same throughout the season. Thus, if a team beats another early in the season, they can lose later because several players are not playing.

The notion about internal and external also applies to saying words such as "believe," "feel," or "sense." Beliefs are not transferable. You can believe something, but just because you do, that does not mean that I believe the same. Few people have the same definition of God, love, patriotism, etc. We need to recognize in ourselves and others that beliefs are internal.

TIME BINDING

The football team example helps us understand the concept of time binding. We know this idea when we consider that an hour is not an hour. An hour at a party is not the same as an hour at the dentist office. Time is complex. There are many types of time, and some of them influence us each day. Our situational concept of time may be referred to as psychological time binding. Two friends of mine were going to meet me for dinner. One of them was from Brazil. The three of us agreed to meet at 6:30 p.m. For my

American friend, that meant that he should be there slightly before or at 6:30. My Brazilian friend thought that meant around 6:30. Even around was somewhat ambiguous for him. After the two of us waited for thirty minutes, we left. My Brazilian friend was hurt because we didn't wait long enough for him. We had encountered cultural time binding.

Time is a cultural concept, and it is probably a subcultural concept. When I first started teaching at a university in Alabama, several of my students showed up for class almost exactly ten minutes late. I had not been used to this tardiness at my previous school. I soon found out that being late was a norm when I went to my first faculty meeting that was scheduled at 10:00 a.m. That meeting and every other one I attended did not start until 10:10 a.m.

Physical time binding is the concept that physical things change, including people. As we grow older, men lose their hair, their hair turns gray, they get wrinkles on their face, and other changes take place. We forget, in this context, that they also change in other ways. We should remember that an argument with a friend may have resulted in serious consequences. I have even known family members who have not spoken to one another for years. Each one assumes that the other person is the same as he was two years ago, five years ago, ten years ago. Most of us change in that amount of time, in many ways. For some, the two in conflict may have forgotten what the original difference was. Thus, we should constantly be in the mood to readdress that which was true before.

We tend to take a sample as the universe of a situation. For example, if I go to a restaurant for the first time, the service may not be good. I tend to assume that the service is never good. However, I do not know that unless I go to the restaurant at least once more. In this way, we discount numerous possibilities. I did ask my students once how many times the men would ask a woman out if she continued to say no. One of the guys in the class raised his hand and answered immediately. He said nine. Nine sounds like too many to me, but bad news once does not mean bad news always.

SPACE BINDING

We see things from a certain point of view. Naturally we can see this when there is a car wreck and there are three witnesses. There are two different drivers and a third witness who was driving another car that was not part of the wreck. Typically, the drivers do not want to admit fault. A policeman might accept the third witness's account as more objective. Of course, it may or may not be a better view. It depends on where she was in relation to the accident. Thus, she is more objective in that she is not involved in the accident, but her perspective may not be helpful because of where she was sitting.

Point of view is more than physical. If a patient has something wrong with his leg, he is likely to get different views from a specialist who deals mainly with bones, or muscles, or veins, or nerves. In a sense we look for what we know the most about. A defense lawyer friend of mine told me that he thinks cops usually first suspect the spouse of a murder. I tend to agree with that. He continued that even when another suspect *confesses,* police want to go back to the spouse. As we were talking about this, I said I thought that we all do this. Our viewpoint is based on memory, experience, and knowledge.

How many times has a basketball player been called for fouling someone of the other team and countered that he didn't do it? The referee saw it. Maybe the crowd saw it. Maybe even his teammates saw it, but he didn't. He could be faking innocence, but it could just be his perspective.

THE USE OF ET CETERA (ETC.)

Chances are that you have heard someone end a sentence with etc. The general semanticists suggest that we should consider the use of this "and others" in our everyday talk. Even if we do not say the words aloud, we should think about what they mean. It simply means that we cannot say everything about anything. Most of our talk involves short cuts. For example, when we greet someone with, "Good morning," we are saying more than that. It means I am glad to see you again. I am glad you are doing all right, and I am doing all right. That's a lot more. When others don't use etc., we can fill it in for them.

THREE QUESTIONS TO ASK

One student of language, Wendell Johnson, developed two questions that he said we should ask in many of our interactions (Johnson and Moeller 1972). The first question was: *What do you mean?* This question helps us determine what we mean or what the other person means by asking for feedback. As we know, "Is it too cold in here?" is not a yes or no informational question. It is asking, "Will you turn up the heat?" or "Do you want me to turn up the heat"? When we try to get a child to do something, frequently we are too subtle. This first question is trying to clarify the difference between what someone is saying and what they mean. It considers the possibility that we do not always say exactly what we mean. Our not doing so can be intentional, it can be accidental, or it can be because we do not know how to say it at that moment. It's some help to the speaker.

When I mention this question to my students, they suggest they would not ask that question because it sounds rude. It probably depends on exactly how we ask it. We could repeat back to the speaker what we *think* she said. Then ask if that is what they are saying. When we do that, we should use different words than the speaker used. The second question may appear even more rude if asked specifically. It is: *How do you know?* In my mind, I would mainly use this question with someone who has tried to share a rumor with me. (I do not like people to share rumors with me because I realize that many are not true, but research indicates there is some truth about each of them.) I might use this question to attempt to quell some conspiracy theory, but that is for another chapter. I would use it if the speaker is saying something unbelievable to me. From a speaker's viewpoint, she may want to start the information with, "Paul, from the accounting office, mentioned ..."

Those first two questions belong to Johnson and Moeller. The third is of my own creation. I was at my faculty office one morning thirty minutes before school started. Like a lot of people, I was there early because it was quiet, and no one else seemed to be there. I could get a great deal of work done in thirty minutes under those circumstances. Suddenly there was a knock on the door. I didn't expect anyone. I opened the door, and I was confronted by a student immediately who said, "You messed me up!" I had no idea what she was talking about. In quick order, she explained that I had signed her schedule for classes a couple of weeks before. She had been assigned a Spanish laboratory in a certain room. She said she had been there four times, and no one was there. I am not certain why she came to me except that she was a freshman, and I was the only person she "knew," because I had signed the schedule. Of course, I knew she could only get an answer from a person in the Spanish department. That is what I suggested after I calmed her down. They fixed her problem.

As it happens, that was a day after I had just finished reading Johnson and Moeller's book. I started wondering what it was about my conversation with my student that bothered me so much. I discovered that it was her inability to target the right person with her question. I developed question three: *Why are you telling ME this?* I have since wondered how many times a restaurant server wondered why a customer was complaining about how long it took to get food. Mistargeting is a communication problem that is rarely discussed. A few years later, I received a telephone call from a stranger. He asked if another person was there. I told him that the person physically worked near our office, but this was not his number. The person on the phone proceeded to start telling me what he wanted to talk to this other person about. I stopped him. He had no reason to tell me this. He was wasting his time. He needed the right target.

Having these three questions in your repertoire is essential for better communication. You may get mistargeted. You may mistarget someone else. You may want to know where their information was found. And certainly, you need to know what they mean. These questions indicate that we are not that great at communicating. General semanticists agree. Many scholars and authors agree too.

LANGUAGE INTENSITY FOR PERSUASION

Most words have synonyms that create different levels of intensity. A vehicle, a car, and a limousine have similar meanings, but vehicle is more general, a car limits the vehicle, and limousine further limits car. A protest, a strike, a revolt, and an insurrection are similar, but some may be used to increase the verbal volume more than others. In persuasive situations, a speaker is likely to use a stronger word.

Let's take these words: dissention, protest, revolt, riot, insurrection. Which word is used should reflect the significance of actions that were taken. However, it is more typical for one side of the issue calls the action one thing, usually on the extreme. For example, a biased speaker might use "riot" for a march. The opposing side of the issue being protested takes the other word on the other end of the spectrum. By increasing the intensity of language, the attempt is to persuade others to your side. A terrorist and a freedom fighter might be the same person simply described differently. In the United States, we seem to use "liberal" and "conservative" to mean a host of things, which would not necessarily be consistent across issues.

SWEARING: CURSING AND BLASPHEMY

Two Ukrainian researchers surveyed college students to determine why they cursed. Babusko and Solovei (2019, 114–15) found that younger students said cursing gave them an emotional relief (40 percent), to shock people (19 percent) and to clarify with emphasis (13 percent). The senior students had a similar emphasis on emotional relief, but they added it was used to show contempt (45 percent). Certainly, these reasons are factors, and they also relate to Americans. However, one of the major factors here is simply habit. Curse words are used interchangeably with other words. Those who use curse words habitually use them as "fill ins" to avoid silent pauses. So "damn," and "hell," and so on replace "uh," "like," and "you know." Johnson and Lewis (2010) found that cursing in meetings and public situations is seen as more unexpected than in private settings. They also found that strong expressions such as "fuck off" were seen as "more unexpected than others like "oh shit" or "that sucks" (115). Other researchers have found similar results. A colleague of mine undertook research to determine what the worst words are. He found that blasphemy was viewed as worse than even the highest intensity word with a sexual connotation.

My experience is that most people use curse words for one of three reasons. One is the aforementioned habit. Certainly, many people regularly use "damn," "hell," and "son of a bitch." Others may regularly use stronger words. The second reason is for the shock value. The person is trying to grab attention. Third, people add curse words to add intensity to what they are saying or feeling, especially in a moment of anger. Facial expressions of anger, high volume, and cursing seem to go together almost always when a person is mad. The impact of swearing depends on the situation. One-on-one communication is one thing; public situations are another. How well you know the person is another factor. The number of people present of a particular gender affects how the listeners analyze swearing.

WUSSY LANGUAGE

Many people, mostly men, believe that using inappropriate language has a macho connotation to it. I know of no research to support that. Many believe that swearing shows a lack of vocabulary in the speaker. I have known soldiers and I have known college professors, and in some I heard no difference in the amount of swearing. At the opposite end of the gender spectrum is what we might call wussy language. Although this language includes the choice of words that a person uses, it also features a general lack of commitment to what the speaker is saying. It is waffling; it is not taking a position. In general, people who speak this way do not offer much to the listener. The listener must *feel* the commitment of the other person, which is not likely to be there. Politicians use wussy language quite frequently.

People who use wussy language are being political whether they are politicians or not. The disadvantage is that you lose a certain amount of power in the interaction when you use wussy language. There are certainly arguments by experts about someone can persuade in this instance. The answer is probably that it depends on whom you talking to. We are back to the situation.

A NOTE ON POLITICALLY CORRECT LANGUAGE

This way of talking is based on the idea that we shouldn't hurt other people's feelings. I agree. However, I have difficulty buying into one person or group deciding what is politically correct and what is not politically correct. Most everyone I know would agree that we should not use explicitly racist, chauvinistic, or homophobic words or sayings or jokes. There are times, though, when I hear that a person has been accused of such things, and I am convinced the accused didn't know something was racist. I am not saying that necessarily makes incorrect or inappropriate language acceptable. What I do think is that we need to educate the person rather than condemning them to hell.

A NOTE ABOUT REDUNDANCY

From about the third grade through my sophomore year in college, I learned that redundancy was a bad thing. I suppose if I am writing in certain genre, that may be true. In oral communication contexts, it is not true. My parents used to say, "If I have told you once, I have told you a hundred times." Probably not a hundred, but they were right about lots of times. I had not adhered to what they were saying. Maybe I forgot.

In today's world there are so many distractions that redundancy is a necessity. I know people who hear but do not listen to what I am saying. This is obvious when they say back to me a couple of the words but not the whole sentence. Their ears were working fine, but their mind was not listening. They were observing something else or using their cell phones. Some redundancy is a good thing.

Too much redundancy is a bad thing. Repeated redundancy is a control device. Repeated redundancy is an attempt to manipulate. Even small children know how to do it. When they ask, beg, cajole, and request for a cookie the fifteenth time, they usually get a cookie.

OVERVIEW

The words we use are important. We have heard, "Sticks and stones can break my bones, but words will never hurt me." To some extent, general semanticists agree with that. The truth is that words *can* hurt others. What we need to do is look at the effect of words from an offensive (as the speaker) and a defensive (as a listener) viewpoint. As a speaker, we need to be careful to be as explicit as possible without hurting the other person. As a listener, we need to try to remember that not all people evaluate and utilize their own language that carefully. Sometimes we merely need to let it go.

CHAPTER 8

WATCH ME IF YOU CAN: FACIAL EXPRESSIONS AND FEELINGS

One of the factors that we always like to know when we are with another person is how they *feel* about what they are saying. If the other person is happy, how happy is she? We know from watching television quiz shows that winners make it pretty obvious how they feel. When a competitive sports team wins a championship, we know how the fans feel. They yell, they jump up and down, they smile, they high-five one another, they hug each other, they kiss each other. Those kinds of exaggerated feelings are obvious.

There have been hundreds of studies about facial expressions going back at least fifty years. Not only do communication researchers look at how feelings are demonstrated, but also psychologists, businesspeople, poker players, spies, lawyers, and others use their knowledge to figure out the personal thoughts of others. The idea that any of us can read a person like a book is simply not true, but there are cues that give us hints about how a person feels or doesn't feel.

Because facial expressions are so key to the concept of empathy here, perhaps we should discuss them. When my daughter was an infant, she was apparently very aware of feelings. I came home one night and picked her up. As I was holding her in my arms, she took her small hands and tried to move the ends of my lips up to look like I was smiling. I had had a bad day. I guess I didn't look happy to her, but she was trying to make me look happy by literally putting a smile on my face.

I taught public speaking when I was a graduate assistant. One of the students in my class had a severe stuttering problem, at least when delivering a speech. A five-minute speech for her might be only four or five sentences. As the speeches got longer, her difficulties continued. I tried to empathize with her giving her positive nonverbal feedback, but I was concerned that the other students might be embarrassed for her. That is not what happened. The other students tried to help her "pull out" the words. They were listening carefully. They were sitting, leaning toward her to help. She finished the course in fine shape, and the rest of the class learned quite a bit about empathy.

I watched the first *Rocky* movie. When Rocky was boxing, I watched the audience in the movie theater. When he was trying to hit his opponent, the audience members were trying to do the same. They were ducking. They had their fists clenched. I am sure their muscles were as tense as his. Movies are good at bringing out our empathy. They can help us to get angry when a character in the movie gets angry. Movies can even make us cry happy tears and sad tears.

A psychologist from the Netherlands has studied empathy in a much more scientific manner. Christian Keysers (2011) had subjects to participate in an experiment. First, he would have one of them hold his hand out, palm up. Then the researcher hit the subject's hand with a paddle. The subject responded just as you would think, showing pain verbally and nonverbally. Next, Keysers had the first subject observe as he did the same to a second subject. The first subject made similar verbal and nonverbal behaviors when the other person was hit by the paddle. So, if we know what something feels like, we feel it when it happens to someone else. Empathy. Keysers thinks that empathy is found in part of the brain. Other communication researchers believe there may be an empathy gene. In any case, the concept of empathy is somehow inherent in our formation. I must say, though, that this does not mean that all of us have the same degree of empathy. Nevertheless, one of the flashes we look for to empathize with is facial expression.

One of the more prominent researchers of facial expression is Paul Ekman (Ekman and Friesen 2003), a psychologist who taught in California. His research took him to many countries over decades to determine what facial expressions are universal (Darwin 1998). Some expressions are limited to certain geographical locations and within certain cultural groups. Those we will discuss here are considered by many to be universal. Ekman has indicated that there are at least seven of these expressions of emotion.

They are happiness, sadness, surprise, fear, anger, disgust, and contempt.

It should be noted here that not everyone is aware of his or her own facial expressions. Many times, we try to cover up how we really feel in a particular situation. There are times, though, when despite our trying to cover up, we "leak" what we really feel. This notion is like a "tell" in poker. Of course, when playing poker, the players always try to cover up how they feel. Here we will discuss the seven emotions that Ekman has written are universal.

HAPPINESS

Perhaps the most obvious and the most positive of the emotions expressed in the face is happiness. Charles Darwin (1969) was also a proponent of several universal emotions and referred to happiness as joy. Synonyms were high spirits, tender feelings, and cheerfulness (Darwin 1969, 370). He even suggested that several animals show happiness. In other animals, it may occur through wagging the tail or "smiling."

Ekman (2003) has written that there are two routes to happiness in humans. One is pleasure, and the other is excitement (Ekman 2003, 100). There are cases when both occur at the same time. For example, when you eat some food that is especially tasty, you may smile and show a positive expression. Eyebrows are up. Various pleasures may lead to happiness. You show excitement when you win a game or an election. It may be accompanied by loud sounds. Again, you show happiness. Cheerleaders are good examples of people showing emotions when their team is winning, stimulating fans to join them in illustrating happiness. When their team is losing, they tend to be quiet until the situation gets better.

SADNESS

The emotion of sadness is the opposite. It is often confused with depression. There is more silence with sadness. Sadness is related to psychological pain. The lips are in an ends-down position. With emoji, we see the emotion of sadness as looking like the opposite of happiness through the position of the lips.

Figure 8.1 Happy and Sad Emoji.

SURPRISE

Surprise occurs when the unexpected happens. If a person is working in a convenience store at night, and a customer with a mask and a gun comes in to rob the store, the worker will feel surprise and fear. Should this sequence occur frequently, the worker may feel surprise and anger. A birthday person surprised by a party may show surprise and happiness. In these cases, surprise is one emotion blended with another. Thus, we have surprise-happiness, surprise-fear, surprise-anger. Each one is somewhat different, but generally the eyebrows are high and curved. The forehead is wrinkled. The mouth is usually open enough to see the person's tongue. The raised brows are the most distinguishing feature.

Figure 8.2 Surprise-Happiness Emoji.

FEAR

Fear and anger are negative emotions. They are often triggered in the same way. For example, if a young child ran into the street to chase a ball, the parent's internal emotion is fear that the child will be harmed. However, as the parent chases the child chasing the ball, that fear is replaced when the parent sees that the child is not hurt. Then anger is targeted to the child in words such as, "How many times have I told you not to run into the street?" Fear is probably the strongest emotion that we show, although Denzin (1984) calls it inauthentic. Certainly, Denzin is right in that fear is short term. That is, any one fear is short term. An emoji can show our stereotypical notion with the wide-open mouth and the eyebrows slanted in toward the nose. The eyes are wide open and bulging. These stereotypical qualities can certainly be the case, but they are more typical of *strong* fear emotions. In those cases, we can feel our hearts beating faster.

Figure 8.3. Fear Emoji.

ANGER

Anger can occur because of several different reasons. It can be because of a blockage to some goal you wish to achieve. If you are watching an important game on television and the cable or electricity goes out, you may become angry. In this case, you are mad at an inanimate object that has interfered with another inanimate object. Anger is often caused by frustration. As we grow, we learn that we cannot get mad every time we are frustrated. Even so, a little anger may show in our nonverbal communication.

We often try to cover up our emotions if we can in a social situation. Small versions of fear and anger, though, seem to seep out even when we try not to show them. An anger emoji shows that the mouth is open with lips down (like a sad face) Often the teeth are exposed in a "hard" fashion as if gritting their teeth. The eyebrows are down toward the nose. In some ways, the fear expression and the anger expression are similar. As it happens, some psychologists have indicated that the brain is functioning similarly for these two emotions. Antonio Damasio asked subjects to think about a story where they felt happy, sad, angry, or afraid while he took a PET scan of their brain. The areas of increased and decreased activity were quite similar (Restak 2001).

Figure 8.4. Anger Emoji.

CONTEMPT AND DISGUST

My most significant memory of the contempt expression is when my son was about three years old. He was really a great kid and still is, but one event showed me what contempt was. I had asked him to do something. He stood right in front of me at his short height. He pointed his finger toward me and shook it while he said, "You don't tell me what to do!" The juxtaposition of his size and his message allowed me to have only one response. I went into the next room and laughed as quietly as I could. Was he serious? He appeared so to me. Apparently, he had learned that line at preschool. But that was contempt. Adults are usually low key about expressing contempt. Sometimes another person catches them rolling their eyes. Contempt could be the motto of teenagers. A wrinkled nose is probably the most common expression found in the face for disgust. Think of some food that you dislike and pretend to see it or smell it, and you will have a disgusted look on your face.

COMPLEXITY OF FACIAL EXPRESSIONS OF EMOTION

Most of us know that determining what someone else is feeling is often difficult. We must remember that as we analyze them, there are other factors that have an effect. Usually, they are consistent with one another. For example, the contempt my son showed me was mostly in his finger pointing, not in his facial expression. He did look like he meant it. He was also loud.

In summary, happiness is expressed not only by a smile but also by a general openness in the hands and arms. Fear and anger are seen in the eyes. There is also often screaming with these feelings. Anger includes not only the loud screaming but also the use of curse words. There is a certain amount of heat included when we consider anger. As an angry argument continues, the symptoms increase. The physical factors are part of why it is so difficult to reduce tension. Sadness is associated with depression. We cannot always tell if someone else is depressed. We need a lot of information to do that. We can tell when they look sad. Their eyes are focused on the ground in many cases. They don't want to talk. When they do talk, their volume is quite low. While researchers disagree about facial expressions, many agree that these expressions are universal, or they are used in a substantial number of cultures.

Eye contact is an important element in communicating with others. In public speaking classes, the teacher usually tells the students that they must have eye contact with the audience to succeed. I used to teach that, but I have learned that there are some problems with that as a universal statement. For one, some cultures and subcultures do not like to expose themselves through their eyes. The other is that having eye contact when you are talking is not natural. However, we should have eye contact with a speaker when we are listening. We should not be looking at the phone, the door, someone else, or the clock. It is essential to have eye contact as a listener, without distractions.

BODY LANGUAGE WITH THE HANDS AND FEET

As we have discussed, the one thing most people want to know about body language is whether the other person is telling the truth. Research consensus is that we cannot tell by their eyes. Professional poker players are good at disguising how they feel about their cards. There are factors that might help you know a little better whether another person is telling the truth. How long have you known them? Do they have a "tell" that lets you know? Do they talk more or less when they are lying? When I first studied the issue of nonverbal communication and truth telling, I thought about courtrooms where it is important to know whether a witness is telling the truth. At that time, the place where researchers agreed you could tell was the feet. The foot movement. I thought about the witness box in most courtrooms. You can't see the leg and foot movement of the witness. Despite the research conclusion that leg and foot movement was the key to determining whether one was lying, I knew you couldn't see them in court.

In fact, no nonverbal gesture is recorded in court. The transcript is written. Some states have toyed with videotaping testimony, but it has not become a popular approach. The courts, then, determine truth by the words that a witness uses and the witness's answers to questions from the lawyers on both sides.

What do we know about gestures? We know that every culture has some sort of greeting. We may not have paid too much attention to that prior to COVID-19, but we certainly have since. Traditionally, acquaintances shook hands as a greeting. Fist bumps were used by some subcultures and groups. Other countries even kissed one another on the cheeks. With the advent of social distancing because of the virus, nonverbal greetings moved more toward short-distance waves. In previous times, the kind of greeting was related to the closeness of the relationship and the amount of time the two parties had been away from one another. In fact, among men, how tight the handshake was between them and other people is an important element of credibility. The COVID-19 virus has had substantial repercussions on greetings. Handshakes and hugs have been virtually eliminated. This "coldness" that became a factor in greetings and farewells may be with us for a while.

Other hand gestures are used to communicate. Some professions use them frequently to send codes to one another. Hand signals are used by the police to move traffic. Airport workers use them to park airplanes. The stock market uses them to sell and buy stock. We use them to let others know it is time to leave. While we use our heads to shake and nod to indicate yes and no, we use our hands, with palms up and shoulder shrug to show we don't know.

These hand, head, and foot gestures tend to vary by culture. Unlike facial expressions, other gestures can easily be seen to be different. Obscene gestures, like "the bird," vary substantially from place to place. The middle finger up is common in the United States. Obscene gestures are even different in different parts of the country. New gestures are invented frequently to be an "inside joke" about obscenity.

OVERVIEW

The ability to "listen" to facial expressions is crucial for improving your communication skills. At least in our country, seven facial expressions are the most common. People may want to add depression, for example, yet it is difficult to distinguish depressed from sad. The ability to recognize expressions is important in your mission to understand what other people mean. Just as with words, we should ask ourselves, *What do you mean?* with our gestures.

CHAPTER 9

I HEARD WHAT YOU SAID, BUT WHAT DID YOU MEAN?

MOTIVE ATTRIBUTION

Although I had been teaching communication for decades, one of the more important elements of the concept of communication did not come to me until recently as I drove home from school. There was a turn. Right after my turn, another driver veered into my lane. I thought I had the right of way, even though there is no legal indication one way or the other. I noticed the first two digits (which indicate county) on the license plate of the automobile driven by the other person. The number was the same as my county. I was irritated. The driver of that car must have known that I had the right of way because he surely had driven there many times. I didn't blow my horn although I really wanted to do so. After that happened, I realized that I encountered this sort of thing on a regular basis. About a week later, a driver with an out-of-state car did the same thing to me. I convinced myself that his behavior was all right because (in my mind) the driver probably did not know any better. So I was thinking not so much about the violation as I was the motive. I assigned different motives to the two drivers simply because I assumed they had different levels of knowledge about the right of way.

My guess is that most of us engage in these kinds of intrapersonal communication (thinking) on a regular basis, but maybe we don't stop to take stock of what we are thinking and consequently doing. I have learned that given the same situation, I can interpret it as the other person did something to me or for me. What this says is that I can assign the motives of the other person in my mind. I do assign motives to other people. So, if both the sender of a message and the receiver each assign different motives, the result may create several problems. My analysis of this can be seen in a simple nonverbal exchange.

I am jaywalking across a street. Someone driving a car honks their horn at me. If I am feeling that the person is berating me for violating the law, I may send him an obscene hand gesture. But if I think this is a friend honking, "hello," I return a friendly wave. The older we get, the better we think we are at analyzing the tone of the honk, so to speak. For example, if there is a long, "hard" honk, we interpret it to mean that they are sending us a negative message of some sort. Two short toots are friendly or friendly reminders that the light has changed.

The attributions we make frequently involve scenarios. We may give another person credit for being too old to drive or too young to drive. We may even give them credit for the time of day or night. But it's just as likely we might critique them for texting while driving or eating while driving. Just the other day, I saw a driver brushing her teeth while driving.

Nevertheless, the importance of these scenarios is that we try to enter the minds of other people as we decide whether to interact with them or how to interact with them. On many occasions, the internal, intrapersonal "self-talk" is the end of the line. We have, in essence, decided that the interaction is complete regardless of what the other person had to say. In fact, they said nothing. They just acted in some way, and we completed the conversation with ourselves.

There are other occasions in which we publicize our attributions to others. Frequently this happens with a third party. How many of us have been having a conversation with someone about a mutual friend? If the other person criticizes the friend, we attempt to end the conversation with, "Well, you know Bob, that's just the way he is." This is an artful way of supporting an absent member while neither agreeing nor disagreeing with the criticism per se.

Most frequently, though, we move in other directions. Once we have assigned a motive, then we can decide how to analyze the message. The important aspect of analyzing a message is to determine whether or not what the other person is saying is interesting—will it draw my attention?

If it doesn't, the likelihood is that the message passes us by, or we ask the other person to repeat it. Various distractions cause us to ask the other person to repeat themselves. One of the primary ones, though, is that we never listened in the first place.

IS IT TRUTH OR BS?

This area is the most important in many conversations. We want to know if the other person is telling us the truth. For whatever reason, we believe that a relationship cannot survive unless the parties are being truthful with one another. Postman and Weingartner (1969) even indicated that one of the most important things that education is supposed to give us is the ability to "detect crap," in their terms. It appears there is quite a bit of crap to detect in our world today.

What exactly we mean by all of this varies. When we say "trust," that means not cheating on one another in dating and marriage. When we elect a president, we expect that person not to cheat on the country. But trust also seems to mean to be reliable. For some partners, that means answering your cell phone immediately. For others, that means showing up on time for dinner. For businesses it means not cheating on money issues either in the company or with the customers. For most of us, it means that the other person is performing the way they really are. It means being predictable. We may enjoy spontaneity in some situations, usually we prefer predictability. What we usually mean is that we want the other to be authentic, which includes most of these issues. That may be hard to do. In other research, I have suggested it means the desire for the other person to be authentic. Authenticity is difficult to define and difficult to detect because it may take a long time. In essence, with people close to us, we only know they were not authentic when they prove to be inauthentic.

A colleague of mine of has written research saying that most people rarely outright lie. For example, if I say my wife's dress is beautiful and it isn't, that lie doesn't count. Numerous others which most of us would say is a lie fall into the category of what he would say is not a lie. He might say that I am being inauthentic when I tell a fib like that. People tend to be deceptive out of some fear that something bad will happen to them should they tell the truth.

PROPAGANDA AND BS

Because truth telling appears to be so important to us, many people have studied it for a long time. We can certainly trace the study of propaganda to 1939 (Lee and Lee 1939), and we know that scholars have become better at detecting it over the years (Pratkanis and Aronson 2001). I bring up propaganda here because many of its techniques are practiced in everyday life by politicians, lawyers, salespersons, advertisers, and others. It is used in everyday conversation. For that reason, we will discuss some of the devices that people use to con us. What we might call "false persuasion."

Propaganda devices are used to shortcut the brain of the hearer. They are false logics. Different propaganda experts list various devices, but I am going to discuss only eleven of the more significant ones that we find in mass media, which are used also in interpersonal communication.

Ad nauseam is repeated repetition. If you watch television, you know about repetition. At times, the same advertisement is shown several times within a thirty-minute program. Repetition is a good system for teaching and instruction. When it is used for persuasion, it is a much more dangerous device. We need to learn for ourselves that just because something is said many times, it is not necessarily true or correct. This caution is the case with people we know as well as strangers. Other people often think they know us better than we know ourselves. That may be the case at times, but not always. Part of resisting BS is resisting repetition.

Appeals to fear are quite often used in numerous contexts. Many salespeople will say that if you don't buy something right now, you may not be able to get it later. I have even noticed on Amazon products that there is "only one left." After that one is sold, there is "only one left" again. One method of fearmongering is trying to force into a quick decision. Shortcut persuasion techniques often seek those who are likely to make a quick decision. A book on Amazon is one thing, but much bigger decisions are made out of fear. In times of crisis, such as when a loved one has died, funeral directors often try to sell the most expensive plan because they know a quick decision is necessary. Insurance people can only sell life insurance to people out of fear about what the customer's family will be able to do without him. Even friends may "scare" you into not having dessert because you fear you may gain weight. Cosmetic companies, clothing companies, deodorant and breath mint companies scare you into buying their products because you fear being unattractive.

There are much bigger examples as well. In 1999, there was an international scare that computers and electronic devices wouldn't work on January 1, 2000. We are asked to believe a nuclear war could happen at any time. COVID-19 scared some people into dangerous actions. And, of course, politicians try to scare us all the time.

Cherry-picking is a little less significant most of the time. Cherry-picking is used when the other person is arguing for something and using only those arguments and facts that support their views. The way to counter this action is by using your counterarguments and the facts that they omitted. My brother and I were arguing once about Social Security. He started by saying that he was against taxes in general, and I took the opposite position. He said that we should handle things ourselves and not pay the government to pay for things. He and I were both getting Social Security checks, so I asked him about that. He said that he had paid for what he received. I told him that he indeed had not. If he were to investigate how much he paid over a lifetime, he would find that in just a few years he had exceeded substantially in what he and his employer (in his case, the government) had paid.

Exaggeration is when a person talks about a person or event to make it seem more significant than it really is. In addition to people doing this in everyday communication, we see it often in politics and in the media. The term "Breaking News" has become so trite that it has lost its meaning. When we inflate a situation, we have exaggerated. We misrepresent the importance of a variety of things in life. If a football team loses a game, a fan might call it so important that the team can never recover. The same can be said of a win, when the fan puffs up about how now the team is going to win a championship.

Half-truth occurs when a person starts a conversation with information that is accurate, but later uses some distortion to end in a falsehood. This technique is often successful in that some listeners are unwilling to extensively check what they have heard in a conversation, especially if they know that part of it is true.

Loaded language is used to create a more emotional response to a person, a group, or an event. It is used quite often in politics to characterize the opponent. The attempt is to associate relatively unemotional words with negative descriptions. Racist and bigoted language are used in this way to make certain groups seem less valued than others. How important is a topic? Just important or jaw-dropping? Jaw-dropping sounds really important.

Oversimplification is used to characterize something as less complex than it is. The person is likely to use short words (rarely over three syllables). The approach views reality as black and white. It attempts to eliminate any gray areas or ambiguous areas. Oversimplification also has short sentences. It is directed toward an audience the speaker believes is not very smart.

Name-calling is one of those nasty devices we learn in elementary school. Children are called four eyes, shorty, and other derogatory names. Politicians use them in adult life. They call one another liberal or conservative, which should not be derogatory. They often add adjectives such as "Washington liberal" which implies that the person targeted is not only a liberal in Podunk, but he is not really one of the Podunk boys. He has lived in the District of Columbia too long.

Scapegoating reminds me of my twin children. I have been out of a room when something was broken. Both were in the room when the crime took place. When I go in and find that a dish has been broken, I ask who did it. The typical response always was, "I didn't do it!" Each one blames the other. Politicians blame previous administrations for problems that have occurred. The more levels of responsibility there are for taking some action, the more levels of blaming someone else. The motto is: "Who did it? Someone else."

Straw man is the idea that the speaker is making up an argument about something that does not exist. In my state, the governor's latest campaign said that she had kept critical race theory out of the schools in Alabama. Critical race theory has never been taught in the schools in Alabama. She took credit for something that is meaningless. She also claimed to have kept voting on the up and up. No one ever said it wasn't on the up and up. I could say, "I have kept the most ghosts out of Alabama." Straw men cannot be challenged because there is nothing to challenge.

Bandwagon is an approach in which the sender tells us that "everybody" is doing so-and-so. We need to join the crowd before we are left out. Because we live in a democracy, we have a tendency to believe that whatever the majority thinks is the right decision. Of course, that may or may not be the case. Friends may try to get you to join a group they belong to. "Everyone is …" is a real danger because everyone probably does not believe anything.

Lying and deception are the general terms for many of the propaganda devices. We certainly have not listed all of them here. But we know that when a speaker tries to convince you of something that is for his benefit and not yours, you should at least be suspicious. Why is this salesperson trying to get me to buy this car *right now*?

OVERVIEW

While I have discussed negative ways that people can and do use persuasion against us, I do not mean to imply that all persuasion is bad. Quite the contrary, much of it is good. This is how we learn to act. Our parents and our teachers convince us to do this and not do that. Still, we have to be wary of who is sending a message to us and why are they doing it. As we mentioned before, if a spouse asks the question, "Is it hot in here?" we know the likely motive is to get us to turn the heater down. That is not malicious, but we could say it is sneaky.

I have said many times that if you want to persuade a person to do anything, there are two things you need to know about them. One is what do they like, really like? The other is what do they dislike, really dislike? There are more theories about persuasion than I could name, but they mostly come down to liking and disliking. The final element of that is the situation. When you are attempting a relationship, the best use of persuasion will not work if they are not ready to have a relationship. But they and you should watch for BS in all their encounters.

CHAPTER 10

THE MEDIUM IS THE MESSAGE: MAYBE MCLUHAN WAS RIGHT

Fifty-something years ago, Marshall McLuhan (1967) was one of the most popular authors on the planet. His claim was that the media was becoming the message. In the 1960s, there were no personal computers, no Google, no Facebook. We had television and newspapers. There was no cable or Wi-Fi. Many of McLuhan's fans supported his notion as he illustrated how pictures of an event had a different impact on listeners than a written story about the event. In those days, there were recordings and some "live" broadcasts. McLuhan contended a newspaper story about a war, though, was different from a newsreel at the movie theater about the same event. With all the new media we have developed since the 1960s, McLuhan's theory appears to have greater strength. Now we know that the same story repeated on two cable channels, from the same data, appear quite different. I started thinking about what had changed the media from being primarily a communication tool to becoming a persuasive tool.

For several years now, I have considered how television news and commentary is doing. I thought about Walter Cronkite as well as Chet Huntley and David Brinkley. As I thought about those newsmen from decades ago, I recalled that in those years, the "nonfiction" portion of television comprised three or four hours a day. So, what seduced us into watching and listening to today's "experts" 24-7? It was Ted Turner. It has been forty years since Turner founded a cable network with its sights *only* on the news.

CNN created several innovations. On the positive side, it emphasized live international news. On the negative side, CNN has to find advertisers because something or someone had to pay for the high cost of live international news. The worldwide aspect and the immediacy aspect were the positives. But when a media outlet operates 24-7, somebody pays for that. With channels like HBO, it is the consumer who pays directly. With news organizations, it's advertisers.

Principle 1: Thus, the first principle is that cable increased the cost of newsgathering and thus transformed the economic model of television news. Advertising became not just helpful, but essential.

CNN was only one of the cable vehicles that infringed on the traditional, three major networks' (ABC, NBC, and CBS) virtual monopolies over television news and whatever advertising money went along with it. Others, like HBO, were infringing on the fiction portion of television. For the traditional networks, advertising had been relatively unimportant for the newspeople. There had been little competition for news money. The networks claimed that the executives were willing to take some financial losses on news advertising to keep news afloat and "separate" from the entertainment portion.

In short, other broadcasting networks could not or would not compete. As a result, they generated "shortcuts." One of the more interesting ones was to report on another network or newspaper report: "The *New York Times* has reported ..." In my mind at least, that is not news, especially when it concludes with "our network has not verified this." That kind of statement is closer to rumor than news. Minimally, it is unverified.

Another shortcut has been to tease stories for attention. For example, "The president has appointed a new member of the cabinet. We'll talk about that after this." After this commercial, that is. Another attention getter is *breaking news*. In all likelihood, the breaking news was also on yesterday.

I worked in radio in the 1960s. The only breaking news item that came across the United Press wire in those years was the assassination of President John Kennedy. Most of today's stories are *not* breaking news. There have been some, such as September 11 and January 6, but there is no breaking news story every day and definitely not every hour. However, with twenty-four hours to say something, news outlets must have a way to attract audiences for the next five minutes, or hour, or day. The role, then, of television news and commentary has become less altruistic and informative and more commercialized and attention getting.

We add to this formula the rise of social media. Here we have the electronic edition of the *National Inquirer*. A third grader's research is probably more competent. But the social media are replicates of the old conversation on the front porch at its best and lewd comments in the college football dressing room at its worst. The important concern is that television also has to compete with it.

Principle 2: Television news programs must compete with the "free" social media.

The evolution of "sources" makes it easier to generate something for television, although it subjugates the meaning of "source." At a minimum, the process blinds the viewer with such phrases as "a source inside the White House." Even worse, the broadcasters have shortcut that phrase to say, "The White House says." I was taught in English classes that buildings do not say anything. Using "The White House ... or the Pentagon ..." has become quite useful as a mechanism to cover up evidence rather than report it.

On the other end of new journalism is not correcting or leaving inappropriate words in a quote. Journalists' interviews previously attempted to increase the credibility of sources by eliminating the grammatical errors of those interviewed. This was quite common with athletes. Their curse words were typically eliminated as well. Many words that are common on the news now would have never been said forty years ago, or perhaps even fifteen years ago. The media leaves the sources' quotes intact, which then become the news story for another day. The new story is that so-and-so responded "___."

Another shortcut is not really a shortcut so much as a distortion in the use of words. In choosing words for a story, frequently commentators select the more dramatic or forceful (and biased) word as opposed to a more objective word. For example, "he said" or "he charged." The idea is that the more charged term will generate more interest than the objective word.

Many of these shortcuts are used as attention-getting mechanisms. The model runs like this. We need advertising revenue. To get advertising revenue we need viewers. Now these viewers have many choices of where to go for news. We need to get their attention for them to come to us.

Conflict and fear are two excellent mechanisms for attention. And here we go.

Television news commentators misrepresent the qualifications of those who speak. Many are not old enough to know directly about Watergate, but they comment as if they do. As for their "experts," they ask former members of Congress and former security personnel about COVID-19 responses and terrorists. The likelihood of their being experts on both seems unlikely. Their opinions are not extremely valid. I suppose the producers have a list of who might get on the air to talk—they call them, and they talk.

When television personalities interview people, they engage in trying to start conflict. "Don't you think ____ is a horrible person?" That kind of question is not a newsperson's question. And the news commentators exaggerate the interviewee's response: "Senator Blank said that this is the worst situation since the Civil War." Fear is a super attention getter. Interviewers even obviously attempt to put words in the mouths of those they are interviewing. "Don't you think ____?"

Principle 3: Now that attention has been gained through fear and conflict, the news commentators have their audience. They use the audience to get that advertising. If they are lucky, the circle goes on and on. In the process, no one gets the news.

As part of the objectivity, we have heard this quote: "Dr. Fauci told us not to wear masks." If I were to ask a conservative if that's true, they would say yes. If I asked a liberal the answer would be no. Neither are exactly right. Fauci said that at the beginning of the virus war. But he said do not get the masks now (then) as the medical people needed them first. So, by eliminating the context, both sides become irritated with the other for misrepresentation.

Media inflate the process knowing that they can get more viewers the more exaggerated the story is. Some outlets reach for the most apocalyptic story. Or reach for the craziest politician. Or reach for a politician who will say something crazy at least.

In all fairness, I do not know how many "newspeople" on television or producers have a background in journalism. I would suggest few. Either way, it may not be such a bad idea for them to take a look at a basic journalism course book.

The selling of the news is rampant and there are few limitations for what they can say to gain attention and attempt to hold it for thirty minutes, nearly half of which are commercials. These comments are probably as relevant for MSNBC as FOX or vice versa. Objectivity should not be limited to a political party and calling it objective does not make it so.

We can see that the truly basic principle is that as far as the news goes, networks have made decisions that support them being persuaders rather than communicators. Many interviews are filled with loaded questions. Again, this is done because the networks are trying to persuade viewers to take a side or keep a side rather than hearing both sides. Traditional persuasion theory says that you use one side only for two reasons. First, you do it because the audience already agrees with you. The second reason is because the audience members aren't very smart. Networks provide only one side for both of those reasons.

WATCHING TELEVISION

My friends and family accuse me of talking to the television. I cannot disagree with the accusation. In a sense, from my viewpoint at least, I am critiquing television. I am aware of the extent to which we are influenced by this medium and others. I try to talk myself out of that influence while continuing to watch. For the most part, I am not talking about the fictional portion of thirty-minute programs except to make my claim that most situation comedies are not funny. But in these cases, too, we are inundated with commercials. I have attempted to measure the time that a show runs and how much time is spent with commercials or network promotions. This criticism does not apply to the cable groups, such as HBO. The amount of time in a regular program is seven minutes of the program and three minutes of commercials. Over an hour, there is about forty-two minutes of programming. Much of the promotions are teasing. These are statements such as, "Houses on fire in local suburb. Details at ten." At this point, you are likely to go to the internet to find out where this is happening.

I have mentioned advertising several times in this chapter. Perhaps it is a good idea to expand upon what advertisers are trying to achieve. If you see a Budweiser commercial on a sports program, the people at Anheuser-Busch do not expect you to leave your seat immediately to purchase a six-pack. You may do it at halftime anyway. But advertisements are based on connections. That is, if you happen to go to the grocery store, you may be interested in buying beer. If you are interested in buying beer, you may choose Budweiser. Of course, Coors advertises too. The important thing for these advertisements is that you think about beer when you go to the grocery store. If you do, one of them will win.

Reality programs have been popular in the past five to ten years. One problem with reality programs is that they are not real. They are scripted much like any other show. The Kardashians cannot possibly be that shallow. The bachelors and bachelorettes cannot be that naive. Paris Hilton cannot be that much of a dingbat. Game shows are also interesting, and are considered reality programs as well.

Family Feud almost always has one Black family and one white family. Two Black or two white families would be unusual. In addition, one family frequently has a huge lead in points with the last question left to go. The differences are often 220 to thirty or so. Often the team with the lower score, with one question left, wins. The last question is worth so much so that it maintains audience interest. On *The Chase*, groups of contestants frequently get close to winning, but the smart guy almost always wins. On other game shows, the contestants rarely win the big bucks.

In fiction programs, the networks found other ways to save themselves money. They created a little phrase called, "to be continued." With this notion, the producers could use a few minutes of footage twice or more. The cable networks caught on to this early. They created television programs (short movies) that lasted six to ten weeks. The programs would be continued next year. You could watch them week by week or you could watch all of them in one sitting if you desired.

One of the biggest problems for television is that there is no feedback. The only feedback is based on whether people watch or not. Even newspapers no longer print letters to the editor. If they do, I doubt you will find many letter writers who disagree with the editors getting their letters in the paper.

The media have similar problems communicating as do us regular folk. I have been following a former Republican commentator on MSNBC for several months now. I am not commenting on what she says so much as the manner. I find her interviews to be extremely verbose; many times, she answers her own questions in her question. Below is what she asked one afternoon:

> You know, Mike, you and your colleagues have been reporting on some of the questions that DOJ investigators have started asking some of the defendants and they include some of what has been alluded to, what did they hear? and how much of this can be believed that it was what Trump wanted to h__ how much of that is going on behind the scenes? How much of that should be in filings like this? And again, how much of that sort of intersects with the Congressional Committee clearly probing this?

That question has ninety-two words in it. There are several parenthetical expressions, and there are at least three questions in the question. This is an example from Nicolle Wallace, an award-winning journalist who holds two communication/journalism degrees. Hopefully, she had time to prepare in advance. Why not shorter questions? Why not shorter answers? These commentators almost always appear to be in a hurry. That is because they know that the next commercial is due soon. Thus, they have to get in as many words (if not ideas) as quickly as possible. Wallace asks these long, interwoven questions quite frequently, but she is not the only one. Most commentators on cable "news" channels do the same.

ENTER THE INTERNET

I bought my first computer in the early 1980s. I could type on it, and it "recorded" what I typed. I could print out what I had typed on a dot matrix printer (Powell, Hickson, and Franks 2018). In the beginning, the personal computer was, for most of us, a fancy typewriter. Even in the early days, it could move paragraphs around. It could delete sentences without white out. It was pretty fancy, but it was essentially a typewriter. As these "typewriters" became more sophisticated, I could do some basic math and statistical work on them. In some ways, they were typewriter/calculator combos.

The age of complexity continued. We got the internet. The internet became a worldwide, interpersonal television. Each person could have a mailbox, a television transmitter and receiver, and a radio transmitter and receiver in a portable iPhone. The technological changes have been phenomenal. The social changes that have served as the content for these new media outlets have not necessarily been helpful. While we may think of Facebook as a social medium, it is actually an ego medium. Some people spend an enormous amount of time creating themselves for others. Sherry Turkle (2011) has focused on the concept of loneliness that has been created and maintained by social media. I agree with her. I do want to add to it the concept of boredom. I believe that those who use the internet for nonbusiness purposes use it because they are bored or lonely. I think aside from addiction, the same is true for video games. But also, video games have essentially replaced board games.

OVERVIEW

When we think of interpersonal communication, we rarely mention the media. However, the media is part of our everyday lives. Media programs and messages are frequently the bases of interpersonal conversation. In addition, although much of media communication is not interactive, we discuss it and "argue" with it. Television has become a generational medium. Social media is not as social as we might like or think. The information we see on news programs is not as substantial as it might have been decades ago.

CHAPTER 11

EPILOGUE: SUMMING UP

In the beginning of this book, I pointed out that communication is significantly more complicated than it may at first appear. I have pointed out a few of the reasons why that is the case. Nevertheless, most people think they are pretty good at it. Most of the training to improve communication is directed toward helping the student become a better speaker or sender. This book has focused on the other side of the issue. Communication works well when people listen to one another. Listening, though, tends to be complicated as well. Here I am going to suggest a few ideas for a good listener to follow.

First, understand that *listening is done with more senses than just hearing*. The words one says are certainly important, but we also need to watch what the other is saying—especially when they are not saying anything. Hearing is a physical attribute, which seems to get more and more difficult as we grow older. We need to pay attention to how well the other person can hear. Can they hear in one ear better than the other? We need to listen with our eyes as well. If we are not paying attention because of distractions, we will likely miss small but important nuances of others' messages. In addition to our being cognizant of the other person's hearing, we need to be aware of their potential eyesight difficulties.

Should she be wearing her glasses? Is his hearing aid in?

Second, we need to try to *learn the general intent of the other person* as soon as possible in a conversation. As I have discussed, there are three possibilities, although they may not be mutually exclusive. Catharsis requires few words and usually no suggestions in the way of response most of the time. The main response should be to let the other person know that you are listening and that you have empathy with them. You should not give a stereotyped response such as "I understand." Remember you need to let them know you are listening, not just hearing. With communication, you may need to respond in a similar way, but in addition you need to let them know through your feedback that you truly understand by providing questions if you don't understand. If the other person is trying to persuade you, you need to listen carefully. Then ask those three questions in some form. What do you mean? How do you know? Why are you telling me this? The answers to these questions allow us to take one of three perspectives on what we hear from another person.

CYNICAL, SKEPTICAL, OR NAIVE

Most of us have taken all these viewpoints from time to time. If we feel that we have been conned by being naive, we tend to revert to being cynical. Cynicism is a protection for us against others calling us naive. The better choice is probably being skeptical. In this approach, we allow the other person to give us enough information to make that person credible. Persuasion is about trying to get some other person to believe something or to do something. The extent to which we believe them is based on what they say but also how important their topic is for us. We analyze a car salesman more than a bartender. The amount of money involved is part of the situation.

Third, *we function better when we think before we speak.* To quote my son, "That's hard." We tend to speak too early. We respond sometimes so quickly that our comment overlaps what the other person is saying. In that sense, we have interrupted before they finished. They may not have had a chance to agree with you before you disagree with them.

Fourth, we need to *listen to the words that each of us is using.* There are several reasons for doing this. The words that a person uses says something about their knowledge and experience. Words also say something about who the person wants to talk about. The tense is another way that tells us whether he wants to talk about the past, the present, or the future. The voice the other person uses lets us know whether it is active or passive. If they speak in the passive voice, it sounds less important.

Fifth, if there is any doubt about what the other person is saying, *we should use feedback to ask them that very question: "What do you mean?"* Most of us do not say what we mean the first time we say something. It is not rude to ask the question. You can preface your question with, "I'm sorry I didn't get that," or "I'm sorry I was distracted. What did you mean?" Unless it is a conflict, the other person will not mind repeating or rewording.

Sixth, *if you are dubious about where the person obtained the information, we can ask them where they got it.* This question can be a little more threatening. In a sense, you are challenging the person when you ask them how they know. The more specific their answer, the more you know about the person. They may just say from TV. That's not very helpful, but the channel or the person is quite helpful. Quite often people simply do not recall where they got the information.

Seventh, we get to the question of all questions about communication messages. *Why are you telling me this?* Many times, you may just want to address this one to yourself. This is where we can decide if it is a cathartic message, and we don't need to solve the problem for them. This is where we can figure out if they are trying to persuade us to do something.

Hopefully, these suggestions will improve your communication. If it does, it will make your life easier and more profitable and less stressful. With the question, "Why are you telling me this?" remember that there are several questions in that question. Learn which is more important in each situation.

Why are you telling me this? Why are *you* telling
me this? Why are you telling *me* this?
Why are you telling me *this*?

REFERENCES

Addeo, E. G., & Burger, R. E. 1974. *Egospeak: Why no one listens to you.* New York: Bantam.

Babushko, S., & Solovel, L. (2019) "What makes university students swear." *Advanced Education* 13: 112–19.

Berne, E. (1964). *Games people play: The psychology of interpersonal relationships.* New York: Grove.

Berscheid, E., Walster, E., & Bohrnstedt, G. (1973). Body image. *Psychology Today, 7,* 119-131.

Carrere, S., & Gottman, J. (1999) "Predicting divorce among newlyweds from the first three minutes of a marital conflict discussion." *Family Process* 38: 293–301.

Darwin, C. (1998). *The expression of the emotions in man and animals.* New York: Greenwood

Davis, M. S. (1973). *Intimate relations.* New York: The Free Press.

Denzin, N. K. (1984). *On understanding emotion.* San Francisco: Jossey-Bass.

Ekman, P. & Friesen, W. V. (2003). *Unmasking the face: A guide to recognizing emotions from facial cues.* Cambridge, MA: Malor.

Garner, A. (1981). *Conversationally speaking.* New York: McGraw-Hill.

Gladwell, M. (2005). *Blink: The power of thinking without thinking.* New York: Little, Brown.

Goffman, E. (2010). *Relations in public: Microstudies of the public order.* New Brunswick, NJ: Transaction.

Hickson, M. III, Powell, L., & Sandoz, M. L. (1987). The effects of eye color on credibility, attraction, and homophily, *Communication Research Reports,* 4, 20-23.

Hickson, M. III. (2013). The largest whale penis in the jungle and other big things: Toward simpler messages. *ETC: A Review of General Semantics*, 70, 395-404.

Johnson, D. I., & Lewis, N. (2010). Perceptions of swearing in the work setting: An expectancy violations theory perspective. *Communication Reports*, 23 (2), 106-118.

Johnson, W., & Moeller, D. (1972). *Living with change: The semantics of coping*. New York: Harper and Row.

Keysers, C. (2011). *The empathic brain: How the discovery of mirror neurons changes our understanding of human nature*. Social Brain Press.

Korzybski, A. (2010). *Selections from Science and Sanity: An introduction to non-Aristotelian systems and general semantics*. 2d ed. Fort Worth, TX: Institute of General Semantics.

Lee, A. M., & Lee, E.B. (1939). *The fine art of propaganda*. New York: Harcourt, Brace.

Maguire, E. A., Gadian, D. G., Johnsrude, I. S., Good, C. D., Ashburner, J., Frackowiak, R. S., & Frith, C. D. (2000). Navigation-related structural change in the hippocampi of taxi drivers. *Proceedings of the National Academy of Sciences,* 97(8), 4398-4403.

McCroskey, J. C., & Richmond, V. P. (1993). Identifying compulsive communicators: The "talkaholic" scale. *Communication Research Reports*, 10, 107-114.

McLuhan, M., & Fiore, Q. (1967). *The medium is the massage: An inventory of effects*. New York: Bantam.

Milgram, S. (1974). *Obedience to authority*. New York: Harper Colophon.

Molloy, J. T. (1988). *The new dress for success*. New York: Warner.

Molloy, J. T. (1996). *The new women's dress for success*. New York: Warner.

Moore, N-J, Hickson, M. III, & Stacks, D. W. (2014). *Nonverbal communication: Studies and applications*. New York: Oxford University Press.

Morris, D. (1967). *The naked ape: A zoologist's study of the human animal*. New York: McGraw-Hill.

Morris, D. (1977). *Manwatching: A field guide to human behavior*. New York: Abrams.

Nierenberg, G., & Calero, H. H. (1971). *How to read a person like a book*. New York: Simon and Schuster.

Postman, N., & Weingartner, C. (1969). *Teaching as a subversive activity.* New York: Delta.

Powell, L., Hickson, M., & Franks, A. (2018). *#Media: A history of media in America.* Dubuque, IA: Kendall Hunt.

Pratkanis, A., & Aronson, E. (2001). *Age of propaganda: The everyday use and abuse of persuasion.* 2d ed. New York: Freeman.

Restak, R. (2001). *The secret life of the brain.* Washington, DC: Dana and John Henry.

Rogers, C. R. (1965). *Client-centered therapy: Its current practice, implications, and theory.* Boston: Houghton Mifflin.

Rudder, C. (2014). *Dataclysm: Who we are when we think no one's looking.* New York: Crown.

Sachs, O. (2010). *The mind's eye.* New York: Vintage Books.

Sellers, H. (2010). *You don't look like anyone I know.* New York: Riverhead Books.

Stacks, D. W., Hill, S. R. Jr., & Hickson, M. III. (1991). *Introduction to communication theory.* Fort Worth, TX: Holt, Rinehart, and Winston.

Tannen, D. (1990). *You just don't understand: Women and men in conversation.* New York: Morrow.

Turkle, S. (2011). *Alone together: Why we expect more from technology and less from each other.* New York: Basic.

Zimbardo, P. (2007). *The Lucifer effect: Understanding how good people turn bad.* New York: Random House.

Zunin, L., & Zunin, N. (1972). *Contact: The first four minutes: An intimate guide to first encounters.* New York: Ballantine.

ABOUT THE AUTHOR

Mark Hickson is a native Georgian. He completed his bachelor of science and master of arts degrees at Auburn University. He graduated from Southern Illinois University with a doctor of philosophy degree in speech. He also completed a second master's degree at Mississippi State University and a JD degree from the Birmingham School of Law in Alabama. He taught at those universities as well as The American University, the University of Alabama at Birmingham, and a university in Bangkok, Thailand. He has coauthored a number of textbooks and other academic books over five decades. He has won regional awards for service, teaching, and research. He has also won a national award for research from the National Communication Association.

OTHER BOOKS BY THE AUTHOR

Hickson, M. III, & Jandt, F. E. (Eds.) (1976). *Marxian perspectives on human communication*. Rochester, NY: PSI.

Hickson, M. III, & Powell, L. (2017). *The political blame game in American democracy*. Lanham, MD: Lexington.

Hickson, M. III, & Roebuck, J. B. (2009). *Deviance and crime in colleges and universities: What goes on in the halls of ivy*. Springfield, IL: Thomas.

Hickson, M. III, & Stacks, D. W. (1985). *NVC Nonverbal communication: Studies and applications*. Dubuque, IA: Brown.

Hickson, M. III, & Stacks, D. W. (1989). *NVC Nonverbal communication: Studies and applications*. 2d ed. Dubuque, IA: Brown.

Hickson, M. III, & Stacks, D. W. (1993). *NVC Nonverbal communication: Studies and applications*. 3d ed. Boston: McGraw-Hill.

Hickson, M. III, & Stacks, D. W. (1998). *Organizational communication in the personal context: From interview to retirement*. Boston: Allyn and Bacon.

Hickson, M. III, & Stacks, D. W. (Eds.) (1992). *Effective communication for academic chairs*. Albany: State University of New York Press.

Hickson, M. III, Stacks, D. W., & Moore, N-J. (2004). *Nonverbal communication: Studies and applications*. 4th ed. Los Angeles: Roxbury.

Hickson, M. III, Powell, L., Jones, M., Morse, M., & Nance, J. (2013). *The talking animal: An introduction to human communication*. Dubuque, IA: Greatriver Technologies.

Hickson, M. III. (2006). *A southern fried education: Growing up in school, 1951-2005*. New York: Iuniverse.

Moore, N-J, Hickson, M. III, & Stacks, D. W. (2010). *Nonverbal communication: Studies and applications*. 5th ed. New York: Oxford University Press.

Moore, N-J, Hickson, M III, & Stacks, D. W. (2014). *Nonverbal communication: Studies and applications.* 6th ed. New York: Oxford University Press.

Powell, L., Amsbary, J., & Hickson, M. III. (2016). Talking sports: The role of communication in sports. Dubuque, IA: Kendall Hunt.

Powell, L., Hickson, M. III, & Franks, A. (2018). *#Media: A history of media in America.* Dubuque, IA: Kendall Hunt.

Powell, L., Vickers, J. S., Amsbary, J. & Hickson, M. III. (2009). *Surviving group meetings: Practical tool for working in groups.* Boca Raton, FL: Walker.

Richmond, V. P., & Hickson, M III. (2002). *Going public: A practical guide to public talk.* Boston: Allyn and Bacon.

Richmond, V. P., McCroskey, J. C., & Hickson, M. III. (2008). *Nonverbal behavior in interpersonal relations.* 6th ed. Boston: Pearson.

Richmond, V. P., McCroskey, J. C., & Hickson, M. III. (2012). *Nonverbal behavior in interpersonal relations.* 7th ed. Boston: Pearson.

Roebuck, J. B., & Hickson, M. III. (1982). *The southern redneck: A phenomenological class study.* New York: Praeger.

Stacks, D. W., Hickson, M. III, & Hill, S. R. Jr. (1991). *Introduction to communication theory.* Fort Worth, TX: Holt, Rinehart, and Winston.

Printed in the United States
by Baker & Taylor Publisher Services

Printed in the United States
by Baker & Taylor Publisher Services